WOMEN CAN'T PARK, MEN CAN'T PACK

THE PSYCHOLOGY OF STEREOTYPES

Geoff Rolls

Chambers

CHAMBERS
An imprint of Chambers Harrap Publishers Ltd
7 Hopetoun Crescent, Edinburgh, EH7 4AY

Chambers Harrap is an Hachette Livre UK company

Editor: Carolyn Richardson
Prepress: Becky Pickard
Publishing Manager: Hazel Norris

www.chambers.co.uk

Designed by Chambers Harrap Publishers Ltd, Edinburgh
Typeset in Palatino Linotype and Serifa BT by Chambers Harrap Publishers Ltd, Edinburgh
Printed and bound in Great Britain by Clays Ltd, St Ives plc

The human understanding when it has once adopted an opinion (either as being the received opinion or as being agreeable to itself) draws all things to support and agree with it.

Francis Bacon, 'Novum organum', 1620
(Burtt, 1977)

for Ella, Billy and Eve – the stereotypical perfect family

Contents

Contents

Introduction

Sticks and stones can break your bones, but names can kill you.

Zimbardo, 2008

Prejudice is a negative belief about a particular group of individuals. We all have a tendency to 'prejudge' others and we do this either on the basis of our own past experience or, if that is limited, with the help of ready-made, off-the-shelf stereotypes.

This book is about some of the many stereotypes that we use so frequently in everyday life. When we categorize entire groups of people – for example the Welsh, the Scots, the English, blacks, whites, women, men, students, blondes, fat people and so on – the stereotyping is explicit. Such stereotypes are often seen in the media and form the basis of many jokes. Stereotypes concerning ethnicity, race or religion are well researched and are, quite rightly, frowned upon since they lead to bias and to discrimination – which is one manifestation of prejudice. In this book, I have tried to avoid some of the better researched and more controversial areas.

However, there are other stereotypes that are so much a part of us that we barely recognize them as such. Many of the stereotypes in this book emerge in everyday conversation and are rarely questioned. When we do not know personally or have little concrete information about a particular group it is easy to accept subconsciously the stereotypes that inhabit the minutiae of our world and subtly permeate our language. Most of us slip idly into assumptions about particular groups of people: young men loitering on street corners are dangerous; politicians tell lies; the elderly have time on their hands. Prejudice and discrimination can result.

We might not consider ourselves to be prejudiced, but we prejudge rather more than we realize or care to admit – as this conundrum demonstrates:

> A father was driving his son to school one day when they were involved in a car crash. The father was killed instantly and the boy was taken to hospital for an emergency operation. The surgeon walked into the operating theatre, looked at the boy's face and exclaimed 'Oh my God, my son!' How could this be?

When I presented my psychology students with this problem, only 25 per cent of the class gave the correct answer: the surgeon was the boy's mother. Perhaps you, like them, will be surprised by the fact that your own preconceptions prevented you from seeing the correct answer immediately.

The word 'stereotype' has so many negative connotations that many readers may be horrified by my contention that we use stereotypes so liberally. Many of the following definitions of the word 'stereotype' are negative in the extreme:

- a simplified and fixed image of all members of a culture or group;
- generalizations about people that are based on limited, sometimes inaccurate, information;
- initial predictions about strangers based on incomplete information about their culture, race, religion or ethnicity;
- a single statement or attitude about a group of people that does not recognize the complex, multidimensional nature of human beings.

If you believe that a stereotype is true of all members of the group in question, then stereotypes are both inaccurate and 'bad', as these definitions suggest. After all, there must be some inefficient Germans and some dull redheaded women – and surely not every short man has a chip on his shoulder? Research suggests that nobody genuinely believes that all members of a group adhere to the stereotype. Nevertheless, there might be some truth behind the stereotypes encountered on a daily basis – and if not, how did they arise in the first place? What is the psychology behind them? If stereotyping is generally regarded with such negativity, why does it continue?

One reason why stereotypes have such a bad press is that most are negative: blondes are dumb, students are lazy and so on. However, there are also some positive stereotypes: for example, left-handed people are creative, or religious people are kind. Despite the fact that both negative and positive stereotypes can be accurate or inaccurate, the majority of psychological research has concentrated on negative, inaccurate stereotypes – and often those associated with particular nationalities or ethnic groups. For this reason, people are generally more aware of the inaccurate and negative stereotypes that most educated people dismiss.

Stereotypes are generalizations that help us in our daily lives. They are quick short cuts that we sometimes use to make sense of things – trying to understand from scratch the complexities of our world is a much lengthier process. Even if stereotypes are incorrect, they serve a 'reality function'. When I see a Rottweiler dog, I give it a wide berth. My stereotype of Rottweilers is that they are dangerous: as a result, I am both prejudiced against them and scared of them. The majority of Rottweilers are not dangerous. However, I have limited knowledge of this breed and I therefore rely on the generalized view. It may be that this is helping to keep me safe.

Evolutionary psychologists suggest that stereotyping has given humans an evolutionary advantage over other animals; being able to distinguish quickly between friends and foes on the strength of their appearance alone has enabled the species to survive and prosper. When taken to an extreme, the need to make a rapid assessment of strangers may tip into xenophobia – and it has been suggested that this fear of strangers, or of people different from oneself, may have strong genetic roots. It is possible that humans may be programmed to respond positively to people who are genetically similar to themselves, and negatively to those who are genetically different. However, this is pure speculation. Besides, finding a reason for a prejudice does not make it acceptable.

The power of the stereotype is demonstrated by a famous social science experiment in the late 1960s by Jane Elliot, a schoolteacher in Iowa, USA (Gilmartin, 1987). Horrified by the widespread racism that had resulted in the assassination of Martin Luther King, Elliott brought to her school a book supposedly written by a leading scientist. She told her class of eight and nine year olds that the book described research proving that people with blue eyes were superior to those with brown eyes. As the brown-eyed children in the class began to look uneasy, she told them that this kind of slovenly behaviour was just what she expected of them. She gave each child a label, to be worn for the rest of the day, so that everyone knew for certain who had brown eyes and who had blue.

Over the course of the day, changes in the children's behaviour soon became apparent. Those with blue eyes were attaining significantly better scores in mathematics, vocabulary and spelling than they had previously achieved, and were reading at two grades above their age level. However, the brown-eyed children were performing significantly worse than expected for their age, and achieving lower results than the week before. Their self-esteem had been buffeted and consequently they became sullen and withdrawn. Meanwhile, their blue-eyed classmates were enjoying their new-found supremacy and showing increased enthusiasm for learning; they also began to manifest strongly disparaging attitudes towards the 'inferior' brown-eyed children.

The following day, however, Elliot explained to the children that she had made a mistake – the research actually showed that the brown-eyed children were superior. She swiftly found that both the academic results and the behaviour of the two groups were completely reversed.

Elliot's class were told that it was acceptable to judge people on the basis of eye colour, but the teacher had not told the children to oppress the inferior group; their instinct for this seemed to be innate. It seems that if children are stereotyped, whether positively or negatively, they will behave accordingly – and will be treated by others in keeping with the label assigned.

Another famous study that demonstrates stereotyping and prejudice in children was conducted by Muzafer Sherif *et al.* (1961). Boys attending a US summer camp were assigned to one of two teams: the 'Rattlers' or the 'Eagles'. The two teams then took part in a series of competitive games, which soon developed into fights. Before long, each team started attributing to the other a series of negative attributes and stereotypes: for example 'All Rattlers are cheats', 'All Eagles are bad at sport' and so on. This study illustrates how quickly people begin to identify with their own group at the expense of another.

The psychological effect of labelling people can sometimes be positive but is usually negative. Numerous effects are recognized. Labelling is used to define 'in-groups' (in which we are included) and 'out-groups' (from which we are excluded). Identifying with a particular social group can lead to an in-group–out-group bias, which is the tendency to favour our own kind and denigrate others. Those people who identify strongly with a particular in-group are more likely to be prejudiced against people in competing out-groups. People tend to believe that their own in-group is composed of many different sorts of people but that all members of the out-group are similar: all Russians are spies, all accountants are boring, all youngsters who wear hoodies are dangerous and so on. This is the 'out-group homogeneity effect', which is a classic example of stereotyping. Once conceived, it can be difficult to abort, although the 'contact hypothesis' suggests that increased contact between different groups of people can loosen its hold and reduce prejudice. As people become more familiar with the differing customs, norms and attitudes of out-group members, they will begin to appreciate the group's diversity.

Perhaps one reason that stereotypes persist is that we sometimes see evidence that they are true in our everyday lives. The so-called 'stereotype threat' (Steele and Aronson, 1995) occurs when someone feels so threatened by the possibility of confirming a negative stereotype that they actually *do* perform worse on a task and thus confirm the stereotype (a 'self-fulfilling prophecy'). An obvious example might be a woman who is so conscious of the 'woman driver' stereotype that her driving is impaired when accompanied by a male passenger. The other side of the coin also operates when a negative stereotype denigrates the ability of an out-group and thus people may experience a so-called 'stereotype lift' – a performance boost that occurs when downward comparisons are made with a denigrated out-group. For example, male drivers (the in-group) might actually drive better if reminded that they are considered to be better drivers than women (the denigrated out-group). This 'stereotype lift' does not occur, though, if researchers manipulate the situation so that negative stereotypes are explicitly invalidated or rendered irrelevant to the task in question. This suggests that it is actually the stereotyping itself that affects subsequent behaviour, regardless of inherent ability. Interestingly, research suggests that many people appear to link negative stereotypes to evaluative tests more or less without thinking (Walton and Cohen, 2003).

Women Can't Park, Men Can't Pack is not a comprehensive scientific analysis of prejudice and stereotyping: there are others far better qualified than me to write such a book (see, for example, Lee *et al.*, 1995). This book is written for the general reader who is interested in exploring the psychology behind specific stereotypes. In my view, the widespread use of stereotypes indicates that they deserve at least some consideration, rather than being rejected out of hand. Improved understanding of stereotypes can help us to better appreciate in all their diversity the groups that are being stereotyped. There is, therefore, much to be gained from investigating a selection of stereotypes and highlighting their accuracies and inaccuracies. As a psychology lecturer, I am aware of the inherent dangers of discussing group differences; however, not to talk about them at all can be equally dangerous.

An increased awareness of the stereotypes covered in this book may cause us to question them and could open our eyes to the individual differences that are evident within every stereotyped group – if only we take the trouble to look. We can continue to use the stereotypes that help us in our everyday lives, whilst at the same time examining, debating and questioning their influence: perhaps this will increase our awareness of the dangers inherent in group bias, which can lead to prejudice and discrimination. My main hope is that by examining some of these everyday stereotypes we will better understand some of the groups portrayed. Question every stereotype that you come across. Be aware that stereotyping can lead to prejudice and discrimination. Look at the individual and not the label, and I am sure you will find plenty of surprises concealed within the jungle of prejudice.

Geoff Rolls
Winchester, 2008

Acknowledgements

First and foremost I would like to thank my wife, Eve, who has played a vital part in all stages of the book's development. She has discussed and shaped every piece of writing and has improved the book beyond measure.

When I first sent a proposal for a book to Chambers, I was fortunate that the manuscript landed on the desk of Camilla Rockwood. Camilla was a great help with the earlier book (*Taking the Proverbial: The Psychology of Proverbs and Sayings*) but left on maternity leave before the book was 'delivered'.

Thanks in no small part to Camilla's sterling efforts, the first book proved successful. Now Hazel Norris has taken up the baton and run with it on this second offering. Hazel has been outstanding in all respects, offering guidance and support but also providing me with the necessary freedom to get the book written. It is rare for an author to agree with every decision made by his or her publishing company, but to date I have agreed with all the people working on this book.

The writing process is so much easier if you know that you have good editorial back-up, and I have the support of a freelance editor whom I believe to be the best in the business: Carolyn Richardson.

I am also grateful to Patrick White of Chambers, who agreed to publish this book.

There are various people who have been happy to discuss this book with me on an informal basis. They include Richard Gross, Jonathan Smith, Rick Godwin, Dermot Murphy, Dean Phillips, Ash Jones and work colleagues at Peter Symonds College. I have been amazed and overwhelmed by the support and encouragement received from my colleagues.

There are two other people who deserve a special mention: good friends Vanessa Byrne and Lynn Jones greeted the first book with such enthusiasm that they were practically a publicity machine in the village where I live. Thank you to one and all.

Picture credits

Page 1 © Pictorial Press Ltd / Alamy; Page 7 © Frances Roberts / Alamy; Page 11 © Pat Canova / Alamy; Page 13 © Ben Molyneux / Alamy; Page 21 © Michael Chevis / Alamy; Page 29 © Julie Mowbray / Alamy; Page 34 © Digital Vision / Alamy; Page 39 © 2004 TopFoto / UPP   TopFoto.co.uk; Page 41 © Corbis Premium RF / Alamy; Page 54 © Oleksiy Maksymenko / Alamy; Page 61 © David Crausby / Alamy; Page 66 © ImageState / Alamy; Page 70 © Content Mine International / Alamy; Page 75 © Steve Sant / Alamy; Page 96 © PhotoAlto / Alamy; Page 104 © Chuck Carlton / Alamy; Page 111 © Paul Doyle / Alamy; Page 116 © The Print Collector / Alamy; Page 121 © Content Mine International / Alamy; Page 130 © Bubbles Photolibrary / Alamy; Page 136 © JUPITERIMAGES / Brand X / Alamy; Page 146 © Dinodia Images / Alamy; Page 151 © Steve Sant / Alamy; Page 158 © Alex Hinds / Alamy; Page 165 © JUPITERIMAGES / Brand X / Alamy; Page 180 © Design Pics Inc. / Alamy; Page 184 © 2003 Topham Picturepoint TopFoto.co.uk

Stereotypes

The aggressive shorty

Napoleon and Hitler, Goebbels and Stalin: all aggressive shorties. If you are one of the many people who believe the well-known stereotype that short people grow up from childhood with an inferiority complex and as such develop a chip on their shoulder which is often expressed aggressively, these examples make the case seem watertight: short men feel inadequate and assert themselves through acts

of aggression. Psychologist Alfred Adler (1870–1937) first coined the term the 'Napoleon complex' to describe an inferiority complex that is believed to affect men who are short in stature, causing them to overcompensate in other areas of their lives. In the case of Napoleon, the facts have been misinterpreted: at approximately 5ft 6in, he was not particularly short for his era – he merely appeared so in comparison with the French Imperial Guards, whose height was above average. This fact, along with a great deal of more general research in this area, suggests that 'small man syndrome' does not exist. Nevertheless, the stereotype persists.

With the increasing availability of cosmetic surgery and all kinds of makeovers designed to make us look more attractive, our height may be one of the last aspects of our appearance that we cannot change. Our focus on height verges on obsession – as illustrated by the public fascination with the height of actor Tom Cruise, shown above. But why does this obsession exist at all?

Let's look first at some of the advantages that seem to come with height.

Many studies suggest that taller people generally make more money – for an extreme example, just look at all those US basketball players. Even in the 'real world', however, it seems that an extra inch of height could well result in additional earnings of £500 a year (Heineck, 2004). This trend seems to apply to both men and women. It is often the case that when otherwise identical female twins differ in height, the taller one earns more. What is the psychological basis of this? Can we explain these findings? Does being taller boost people's self-esteem, or is their success the result of the way we treat tall people?

A team of economists from the universities of Pennsylvania and Michigan found that tall men who were short in high school earn the same as short men, whilst short men who were tall in high school earn the same as tall men (Persico *et al.*, 2003). This suggests that self-esteem levels as reflected in salary cannot be blamed on present-day height discrimination; they relate more closely to a person's height in adolescence. The researchers concluded that tall high-school students thought of themselves as leaders in school and were far more successful in extracurricular activities. Since success breeds success, the taller students went on to become the most successful in later life, despite the fact that the shorter adolescents had by then caught up with them in height.

Further support for this stereotype comes from Anne Case and Christina Paxson, economists at the Center for Health and Wellbeing at Princeton University, who published a paper with a blunt and arresting conclusion: 'On average, taller people earn more because they are smarter' (Case and Paxson, 2006). Their research was based on data from the USA and UK, and appeared to endorse findings from other studies that tall men and women earn ten per cent more than those in the same jobs who are 4in shorter. In addition, graphs based on census reports suggest that US men of 6ft 2in are three per cent more likely to hold executive positions than those of 5ft 10in. Again, explanations are rooted in adolescence and the social standing that the men may have acquired, or not acquired, because of their confidence as teenagers. A child who experiences a growth spurt in his or her early teens is more likely to be confident and have greater cognitive ability than one who develops later or less. The researchers suggest that 'as early as age three – before schooling has had a chance to play a role – and throughout childhood, taller children perform significantly better on cognitive tests'. Case and Paxson conclude that:

> Tall children are much more likely to become tall adults. As adults, taller individuals are more likely to select into higher-paid occupations that require more advanced verbal and numerical skills and greater intelligence, for which they earn handsome returns. Furthermore, we show that taller adults select into occupations that have higher cognitive skill requirements and lower physical skill demands.

Case and Paxson, 2006

Both height and cognitive (thinking) skills are influenced by the most obvious and controllable variable of all: nutrition. It is possible that early childhood care, including prenatal care, can increase both height and cognitive ability. Beyond good early nutrition we have little control over height. But with new research claiming that tall people are wealthier and happier – and even, some say, more intelligent – some parents in the USA are already demanding growth hormone injections for their children. Nicola Persico and her team carried out a cost–benefit analysis, which showed that this expensive treatment would more than pay for itself in the potential for increased earnings (Persico *et al.*, 2003). Soon, growth hormone injections may be seen as a perfectly acceptable intervention, like Botox®. But, as Persico points out, if everyone makes themselves taller, we shall have to go to greater extremes to be above average – it will be a case of 'raising the bar' quite literally.

It is not only salary that may increase with height. There is also a relationship between height and the capacity to take on leadership roles – though since leadership roles are often rewarded with higher salaries, the two are closely linked. There are numerous books that report that the taller US presidential candidate always wins – this is not entirely true, although going back to 1928 there have only been four occasions out of 21 elections when the shorter candidate has won (Richard Nixon in 1972, Jimmy Carter in 1976 and George W Bush in 2000 and 2004). Perhaps because US politicians are aware of the Presidential Height Index (which predicts the election result based on candidate height), it is suggested that a number of candidates have exaggerated claims about their height. It might be interesting to look at the height of the heels of their shoes and how this could have confused the voters! It was no surprise to political height commentators that the 6ft 1in Barack Obama stormed to such a decisive victory over the diminutive 5ft 6in John McCain in the 2008 US election.

So much for height as an indicator of leadership potential.

Daniel Nettle of the Open University (Nettle, 2002) reported that taller men are seen as more attractive and as a result are more likely to father children. His analysis of 10,000 people born in the UK in one week in March 1958 revealed that a man of above average height (6ft) was more likely to have children than a man of average height (5ft 10in). Women, on the other hand, were more likely to be married and have children if they were below the average height of 5ft 3in.

So height seems to be an advantage for a man in many respects. But what about the stereotype that small men are more aggressive than taller ones? The Aggression Research Group at the University of Central Lancashire, headed by Mike Eslea and Dominik Ritter, conducted a fascinating experiment to investigate this (Eslea and Ritter, 2007). Ten men below 5ft 5in and ten men of average height participated in a study that tested their physical abilities – such as hand-eye coordination and reaction times – or so they were led to believe ... In reality, they were taking part in a game designed to test their aggression. First, they were seated in pairs and connected to heart monitors. They were then invited to play the game 'chopsticks'. This involved them trying to rap their opponent's chopstick as quickly as possible whilst the opponent tried to dodge away: in effect, they were conducting a sword fight with chopsticks. Unbeknown to the one genuine participant in each pair, his opponent was then asked to deliberately rap him on the knuckles. The experimenters took physiological measures of how the participants reacted to this provocation. Their results showed that the shorter participants were *less* likely to become aggressive than the taller participants, thus refuting the Napoleon stereotype. Mike Eslea concluded that short men are not more aggressive – in fact, the reverse is true. However, when people see a short man being aggressive they put it down to the man's size, since this physical feature is so obvious. The underlying causes of aggression in taller people are assigned to numerous other reasons specific to the situation.

We can safely conclude that the existence of 'small man syndrome', whereby shorties are stereotyped as aggressive, is not supported by the research. Remember Ghandi was only 5ft 3in and you can't get much less aggressive than him. For every Hitler there is a Saddam Hussein (6ft 2in), for every Napoleon there is an Idi Amin (6ft 4in) and for every Stalin there is an Osama Bin Laden (6ft 4in) – all of them tall men, with equally aggressive tendencies. And think of those lovable shorties Ronnie Corbett, Mickey Rooney and Ernie Wise, whom we could hardly call tyrants. Men of short stature do sometimes have the odds stacked up against them – and from their perspective it must seem a high stack. But in reality they are no more aggressive than their taller contemporaries. Perhaps it's time to give shorties a break – and a leg-up on the career ladder.

The aphrodisiac oyster

It is generally believed that oysters are aphrodisiacs, but I'm not so sure. The other evening I ate a dozen – and only ten of them worked.

The joke above is one of my favourites and serves to illustrate what most people believe to be true – that oysters are right at the top of the world's list of aphrodisiacs, best eaten with a lover when romance beckons. The English in particular – despite, or perhaps because of, the fact that they are not known as the world's greatest lovers – have a long-standing affinity with oysters. We have concrete evidence that this dates back many hundreds of years: for example, the diarist Samuel Pepys (1633–1703) declared his love of oysters, both raw and smoked. But can these quirky little creatures really tickle the parts that other shellfish fail to reach?

Giacomo Casanova (1725–98), a rather spicier diarist than Pepys, is chiefly remembered for the amorous adventures described in his memoirs. Casanova must be one of the most high-profile oyster enthusiasts of all time. It is said that he ate 60 a day, and that these sustained him for a lifetime's lovemaking with a total of 122 lovers; perhaps this excerpt will give you a flavour of his taste for both oysters and women:

> I placed the shell on the edge of her lips and, after a good deal of laughing, she sucked in the oyster, which she held

between her lips. I instantly recovered it by placing my
lips on hers.

                                                        Machen, 1894

The word 'aphrodisiac' comes from Aphrodite, the Greek goddess
of love, lust and beauty, who was another famous fan of oysters.
Known by the Romans as Venus, she had no ordinary birth: she
was brought forth from the waves on an oyster shell – although in
the famous painting by Sandro Botticelli (1445–1510), *The Birth of
Venus*, it looks to me more like a scallop shell. Aphrodite, in turn,
gave birth to Eros, who in Roman mythology is known as Cupid.

So what is the origin of the humble oyster's special status? Some
claim that the aphrodisiac qualities of oysters are related to their
appearance – and it is true that, on close inspection, an oyster
resembles the female genitalia. Sexual appetite often begins in the
mind and so, regardless of any physical effects, the mere sight of
an oyster could be arousing to some. Beyond visual echoes such
as this, which may stimulate initial stirrings, one might question
whether aphrodisiacs exist at all? It is often the case that if people
truly believe something to be endowed with special properties, it
will have the predicted result – even if this is due to the placebo
effect. The ground horn of a rhinoceros, the fluid extracted from a
monkey's pituitary gland … all these might act as aphrodisiacs if
people believe that they will. Is it only our blind belief that keeps
our friend the oyster at the top of the aphrodisiac list, or is there
more tangible evidence of his special powers?

An impressive body of scientific support extols the nutritional
benefits of oysters. Firstly, they are rich in the mineral zinc, which
controls progesterone levels. Men are frequently deficient in
zinc, and if levels fall too low, this can cause impotence and a

lack of libido; the zinc that oysters provide can improve male fertility. Furthermore, zinc is found in sperm and men lose between one and three milligrams of zinc per ejaculation. Oysters can, therefore, provide the perfect top-up. Zinc is also a proven immunity booster and may therefore help prevent colds and flu; what's more, it plays a part in the regulation of growth, and helps to keep us mentally alert. *The American Journal of Clinical Nutrition* estimates that most adults only consume about half the recommended daily intake for zinc (15 milligrams). One oyster a day would provide us with almost 100 per cent of our daily requirements. What's more, an oyster also contains omega-3 fatty acids, which are known to help prevent heart disease.

George Fisher, from the Chemistry Department of Barry University in Miami, USA, found by means of high-performance liquid chromatography that oysters also contain rare amino acids – D-aspartic acid (D-asp) and N-methyl-D-aspartate (NMDA) – which increase the levels of sex hormones (Mirza *et al.*, 2005). Scientists from the Laboratory of Neurobiology in Naples had already found that injecting these amino acids into rats resulted in an increase in the production of testosterone in males and progesterone in females. Raw oysters were particularly high in these amino acids. Disappointingly, Robert Shmerling of Harvard Medical School (Shmerling, 2005) throws into question the relevance of these findings, querying whether D–asp and NMDA have the same effects in humans: 'It will take much more compelling evidence – with human subjects', he says, 'to prove a link between seafood and libido.' I believe my wife has already put my name down for future trials ...

Finally, a word of warning. There is a saying that oysters should only be eaten when there is an 'r' in the month – from September to April. This is because oysters may carry the common saltwater bacterium *Vibrio vulnificus* (known to cause muscle aches and fever in vulnerable people), which breeds best in the warmer months. And illness due to seafood poisoning is unlikely to stimulate the sexual appetite ...

➡ *See also* The porn-obsessed man; The sex-obsessed man.

The big-footed man with the satisfied smile

The size of a man's penis has, throughout history and in many different cultures, been seen by some as a measure of his potency and manliness. As a result, most men have at some time wondered how the size of their vital organ compares with that of others – and their partners too may find such conjecture intriguing. Given the widespread fascination that surrounds this topic, the suggestion that we might be able to predict the size of a man's penis without even seeing it is an alluring one that many  are keen to believe. Some suggest that the size of other parts of the body – most commonly the feet – are predictors of penis size (McCary, 1971). Given that my feet are huge, I would be delighted to be able to prove that this stereotype is founded on fact.

Several studies have investigated the topic. For example, Siminoski and Bain (1993) found a very weak correlation between height, penis length and foot size. Edwards (2002) conducted a survey on shoe size and erect penile length among 3,100 men, but found no relationship between the two. However, since both these studies required participants to provide their own measurements their results may be unreliable.

Two urologists working at London hospitals carried out the definitive study on the subject by themselves measuring the vital parts of 104 men who had already been referred to them (Shah and Christopher, 2002). The true length of a penis can only be ascertained when fully erect. However, this presents obvious practical problems and since previous studies had confirmed that flaccid length remains a valid estimator of erect length (Wessels *et al.*, 1996), the researchers decided to make this their prime focus. As any man who swims in British coastal waters will know, the length of the flaccid penis can vary in response to various environmental factors including the cold; therefore all patients were measured immediately on undressing to minimize variations caused by temperature. For those of you who are particularly curious, the penis lengths recorded ranged from 6cm to 18cm, with a median (middle) measurement of 13cm. The correlation between shoe size and penis length was negligible, suggesting no statistical relationship between the two measures.

The researchers concluded that 'the ability to predict the size of a man's penis by observing his shoe size is a common misconception ... there is no scientific support for the relationship'. Good news for all men with small feet. Of course it may be the case that the size of some other part of the body is related to penis length: other possible candidates include hand span, finger and nose length. Jyoti Shah has promised further research on this delicate issue (Shah and Christopher, 2002).

People say you can tell a lot about a man from the clothes that he's wearing but it seems that his shoes cannot tell you quite as much as you might have hoped. A smile of smug satisfaction might possibly be more revealing.

The boorish White Van Man

We've all been there. Driving along the road in a law-abiding fashion, just under the speed limit and checking our rear-view mirror every 20 seconds, when suddenly we catch sight of a white

van looming. Like a bat out of hell, it races up behind us, poised to overtake. At the earliest opportunity, the gears crunch and the van cuts in front, then accelerates away into the distance. And so White Van Man is stereotyped as boorish in the extreme – someone who never signals and always drives with total disregard for others. The stereotype also suggests that he is a tattooed white male, though we are not able to confirm this as he speeds past.

The term White Van Man is thought to have been coined by presenter Sarah Kennedy on BBC Radio 2 in 1997. Although the term can also be used in a non-pejorative way to refer to 'the man in the street', it is used almost exclusively in the UK as a name for thoughtless or aggressive drivers of light goods vehicles. White is often the preferred colour of such vehicles as it facilitates the addition of a logo or name. However, once obtained the van often remains unadorned – possibly since the driver of an unmarked vehicle is less easily identified. We know that White Van Man is likely to be a builder, courier, shopkeeper, electrician, plumber or handyman, and is usually self-employed or working for a small business. Many of us believe him to be the most inconsiderate and unsafe driver on the road. But is this entirely fair? Does every driver of a white van deserve this derogatory epithet?

Since White Van Man is a relatively new species, there has been little research as yet into his characteristics. However, psychologist Ian Walker from the University of Bath conducted an innovative and rather brave study of White Van Man's driving behaviour (Walker, 2006). Walker fitted his own bike with an ultrasonic sensor, which measured the distance that drivers gave him when overtaking. Cycling around Bristol and Salisbury in 2006, he systematically recorded 2,500 incidents of overtaking. The Highway Code advises drivers of all vehicles to give motorcyclists, cyclists and horse riders 'plenty of room' when overtaking, and 'at least as much room as they would when overtaking a car'. However, the results of Walker's research provide robust and significant evidence that White Van Man ignores this advice more than other road users. He found that white vans passed 10cm closer to the bike when overtaking it than did black cars or cars of other colours. Walker concluded that social factors accounting for such behaviour might include a macho subculture, time pressures and the anonymity of driving an unmarked vehicle.

Further research has been conducted by the Social Issues Research Centre (SIRC, 1998, 2003), whose intrepid researchers themselves travelled the country in a white van. They deliberately stopped at the filling stations, industrial estates, lay-bys and service areas where White Van Man is often found, to ask him about his driving habits and views. Their results show that 96 per cent of white van drivers are male; the average age of White Van Man is 37 years, and there is a 60 per cent chance that he is married. If White Van Man is said to behave as if he owns the road, this may be because he is driving around his local area, as typical of 75 per cent of his kind, and he may thus have acquired a sense of territory.

White Van Man listens to local radio (someone has to) and reads tabloid newspapers (ditto), which fit neatly on the dashboard. Unconcerned about his diet, he eats at a 'greasy spoon cafe' or enjoys a filling station 'meal option' of sandwich, crisps and a Coke®. In his spare time he is active, enjoys playing football and has varied interests that provide a welcome contrast to his work. He doesn't go to the pub much, but is likely to own a satellite dish so may enjoy staying in to watch TV. If this all sounds a trifle mundane, don't be too sorry for White Van Man: he holidays in Greece, Cyprus, Spain or Malta and has sometimes been spotted cruising down the Nile (though not in a white van). Even more exciting, he may well have had a 'romantic liaison' in his van.

How does White Van Man view himself? As many as 50 per cent of those interviewed believed that the stereotype is partly justified in the case of *other* white van drivers, but should certainly not be applied to themselves. Nevertheless, 10 per cent admitted to motoring violations and viewed speeding and going through amber lights as a necessary part of the job. Of course, the fact that White Van Man is a better driver than most ensures that he carries out these risky manoeuvres safely – or so he says.

However, 30 per cent of those interviewed rejected the White Van Man stereotype completely. Some put forward sensible arguments to explain the development and maintenance of the stereotype. For example, one bad experience with a White Van Man may cause motorists to tar all others with the same brush. Another possibility is that some drivers *expect* White Van Man to be aggressive and try to get their retaliation in first; others deliberately obstruct him because of his reputation. White Van Man also points out that his higher driving position relative to most car users allows him to 'look down' on other drivers, and for this reason they may find him intimidating.

Let's not be too hard on White Van Man – particularly since he does have some positive characteristics. A study by the Automobile Association (2007) showed him to be diligent and hard-working, with an average annual income of £21,000 – contributing over £35 billion to the British economy each year. What's more, drivers of emergency service vehicles seem particularly grateful to White Van Man, who makes valiant efforts to get out of the way of their vehicles and spots the flashing lights and sirens before anyone else.

Perhaps we are being unkind to White Van Man and, frustrated by our inadequate traffic system, we use his boorishness as a scapegoat for our anger – which we could just as easily vent on some other group of drivers. Where I live, it's Beige Caravan Man who is the menace of our roads in the summer – and frankly I know which I prefer.

The boy in blue and the girl in pink

I have to admit that I've never been brave enough to wear pink. If I were a golfer or a sailor, perhaps the odd pink or pastel striped pullover would have found its way into my wardrobe. But I'm not, and therefore most of my clothes are in manly blue or black. From the moment of birth, it seems that boys are stereotyped as wearing blue and girls are attired in pink. I've got one son and one daughter and, as good psychologists, my wife and I have tried to avoid bringing them up in that stereotypical way. The result? My son is the boy in blue: he loves football and likes to wear a Chelsea shirt each day (only because it is blue, I hope). My daughter is the girl in pink: she plays constantly with her dolls (she has 22 of them) and exhibits a strong preference for pink dresses. Why is this?

Well, despite our best efforts, research shows that most of us, including parents, interact differently with babies dependent on their gender. An experiment by Will *et al.* (1976) demonstrated that adults interact differently with the same baby depending on whether they believe the child to be male or female. In this study, an infant was sometimes dressed in blue and introduced as 'Adam' and on other occasions dressed in pink and called 'Beth'. There were three toys available for the child to play with – a train (boy stereotype), a doll (girl stereotype) and a fish (neutral). Adults were far more likely to give the child the appropriate gender-stereotyped toy, and 'Beth' was smiled at more than 'Adam'.

In a similar study, Smith and Lloyd (1978) arranged for new mothers to play with two female and two male infants. Each baby was dressed in either blue or pink clothes – sometimes according to the traditional stereotype, and sometimes not. Various stereotypical boy, girl and neutral toys were available in the room. Results showed that the mothers tended to choose toys according to the sex suggested by the baby's clothes. In addition, those infants thought to be boys were verbally encouraged to engage in more physical play than the girls. The fact that these differences were evident when different mothers were playing with the same baby suggests that they were not responding to any real behavioural differences between the children. Smith and Lloyd therefore concluded that babies undergo early socialization in the direction of their gender stereotype.

Although we might think that 'blue for a boy, pink for a girl' has a long history, this may not actually be the case. There is some evidence that pink was once considered more of a boy's colour and blue was thought more appropriate for girls. The US *Ladies' Home Journal* (1918) suggested that 'pink being a more decided and stronger color is more suitable for the boy, while blue, which is more delicate and dainty, is pertier for the girl.' Prior to the 1930s, it seems that pink was seen as a derivation of red – signifying power and strength – and was therefore regarded as a male colour. It is only in the last 60 or 70 years that our present colour stereotypes have become the accepted norm.

Colour in general seems to be important to children: for example, they use colour as a deciding factor when choosing objects, food and drinks (Oram *et al.*, 1995). In an intriguing study, Isaacs (1980) asked children to state their preferred colours. He subsequently asked them to catch balls of different colours, only to find that they were significantly better at catching the balls of their chosen colour. Perhaps we should ensure that all the cricketers chosen to play for England have a preference for the colour red.

Advertisers are well aware of the colour preferences of children and parents, and exploit this by using sex-specific colours. Children themselves use the colour of clothes to determine a person's sex, even before they have an understanding of biological differences (Picariello *et al.*, 1990). Shoots (1996) investigated colour stereotyping in children aged between three and five years. She read aloud to the children 50 stories that established a relationship between colour (blue/pink) and sex (male/female). The children were then asked to state their colour preference and what they thought a child of the opposite sex would prefer. Blue was chosen more often than any other colour by boys; pink was chosen more often than any other colour by girls. This shows that traditional colour stereotyping can influence children as young as three years. But would this apply in societies where the stereotype wasn't so strongly emphasized by the media?

Some academics have claimed that women's fondness for the colour pink may not simply be down to 'Barbie® pink' socialization processes – but to evolutionary factors as well. Hurlbert and Ling (2007) asked British Caucasian men and women to select their preferred colours from a series of paired coloured rectangles. The researchers found that the colour that was universally preferred was blue. However, the women displayed a preference for the red end of the green axis: this shifts their colour preference away from blue towards red, which makes pinks and lilacs the most preferred colours in comparison to others. They also tested a small group of Chinese people and found similar results, suggesting that the sex differences may be biological rather than cultural. The difference between the sexes was so clear that the researchers claimed that they could usually predict the sex of participants from their colour choices alone. Ling speculates that these preferences may relate back to the era when humans were hunter-gatherers: those women who chose red fruit to pick may have been at an advantage, since this fruit was ripe. (Not so lucky the women who chose red yew berries or purple deadly nightshade berries, since both of these are poisonous.) Why did both men and women show a universal preference for blue in Hurlbert and Ling's experiment? Hurlbert suggests that blue is associated with a clear sky and good weather – as well as a clean and safe water source. Hence both men and women favour blue.

The assertion that there may be innate biological differences between the sexes in relation to colour preference is controversial. Some feminists believe that the colour pink, dresses, skirts and so forth symbolize the way women are oppressed in modern society. Suggesting that there might be biological factors that account for this is, for them, the final straw – as if science is being twisted to reinforce the stereotype. But perhaps the reason behind it is quite simple and practical, and not sinister at all. Dressing an infant in a gender-appropriate colour tells people whether the child is a boy or a girl – and they are thus spared the embarrassment of getting it wrong.

The brainy first-born

The eldest child is brainy, the middle one difficult and the youngest a rebel – according to the stereotype. Speaking for myself, both my wife and I are youngest children; I am not sure that we are rebels, but we both believe that we are treated differently from and by our other siblings – even as adults.

Stereotypes about birth order persist and abound, but are largely split between two camps. On the one hand there is research suggesting that birth order has a marked effect on intelligence and personality. On the other hand there are claims that all theories concerning the effects of birth order are suspect.

The science of birth order began in 1874 when Sir Francis Galton (1822–1911) revealed that 48 per cent of the 99 famous scientists that he had investigated for his book *English Men of Science* were first-born or only sons. (He ignored daughters, as was the fashion in those days.) Galton concluded that first-borns had a significant advantage in life (Galton, 1874). Some 50 years later, psychologist Alfred Adler (1870–1937) proposed the theory of the 'inferiority complex' (Ansbacher and Ansbacher, 1956). This theory focuses on the fact that first-borns gain the exclusive love, energy and resources of their parents until the second child arrives. With the advent of a new sibling, a first-born suffers feelings of 'dethronement' and a sense of rejection. Adler suggested that this chapter of events can make the older child more susceptible to neuroticism and emotional problems and more likely to fall prey to alcoholism or crime in later life. Younger children, by contrast, are overindulged and spoilt. A middle child himself,

Adler suggests that these children are the most likely to develop into balanced and well-adjusted adults.

Adler's views find little support in published research, where any differences related to birth order usually suggest an advantage to first-born children. So what explanations are given for the first-born's advantage? One explanation is known as the 'resource dilution' model. Each family has finite resources (in terms of time, money and attention) to bestow on its children. First-borns have a period of time in which they have all these resources to themselves, without having to share them with another sibling. An alternative explanation focuses on the possible role of the oldest child as 'teacher' of the younger siblings. One of the best ways to learn is to teach and this may therefore contribute to first-borns developing into leaders rather than followers.

Frank Sulloway, of the University of California at Berkeley, argues that first-borns are more conscientious, less agreeable and less extrovert than later arrivals, who tend to be the 'rebels' of the family (Sulloway, 1996). Research by Kristensen and Bjerkedal (2007) found that first-borns had intelligence quotient (IQ) test scores that were on average 2.3 points higher than those of their second-born brothers. Using IQ tests taken from the military records of 241,310 Norwegian conscripts, they found evidence to suggest that the difference in intelligence was due to the brothers' different 'social rank' in the family. They reached this conclusion by looking at second- and third-born brothers with an older sibling (male or female) who had died in infancy. They found that second-borns who grew up as the oldest child in the family because of a sibling death had average IQ scores equivalent to first-borns. And the scores of third-borns who moved into second place in the family also increased, on average, by one point, bringing them to the same level as second-borns. This may suggest that it is family environment and expectations rather than biological order of birth that account for the intelligence boost. In other words, it is not being *born* the eldest but being *reared* as the eldest that is important.

However, when the data is analysed again, the evidence for first-borns starting life with an advantage seems less clear-cut. One of the most comprehensive studies into birth order effects was carried out in Switzerland by Ernst and Angst (1983), using a sample of 7,582 college-age residents. They investigated twelve different aspects of personality and found no significant birth order effects at all among subjects from two-child families.

One of the most outspoken critics of the birth order effect is Judith Rich Harris, who dismisses the idea altogether. So upset was Sulloway by her criticisms that publication of her book on the subject was held up for four years because of legal threats. One of Harris's main criticisms is that the birth order effect predicts that only children should have an 'intermediate' personality and temperament – somewhere between those of the eldest and youngest – and yet their personalities are indistinguishable from those of their peers who have siblings (Harris, 1998).

If the birth order effect exists at all, it has a negligible effect on personality. You are not destined to braininess or a life of success as a leader simply because you are the first-born child – any more than you are likely to be a rebel if you are the youngest.

The common names of common people

In the 1970s TV sitcom *The Good Life*, the middle-class Surbiton-dwelling female characters were named Margot and Barbara. In the 1990s, the two working-class women in the TV comedy *Birds of a Feather* were christened Sharon and Tracey. Why did the BBC choose these names? Because they fitted perfectly with the stereotypes associated with their respective characters, of course. But which came first? Did the names help to create the stereotypes? Or did the stereotypes influence the choice of the names?

Whilst few of us are required to name characters appearing on TV, many of us have children whose first names we choose. A name may be chosen because of its connotations – because it is a family name, or the name of someone that the parents admire. Or it may be chosen simply for its sound. However it is arrived at, a person's first name is one of the most obvious components of his or her identity and may be the first piece of information that we are given – often before we meet the person. Imagine that you have arranged to meet Britney, Shelley, Apple, Hazel, Diana, Margaret or Carolyn, and give a moment's thought to your expectations. Then select one of the other names, and notice the difference.

The influence of a first name extends far beyond our initial expectations, however. There is considerable research evidence showing that it continues, throughout all our interactions, to affect the way we interpret an individual's behaviour. If our expectations concerning people's personalities or capabilities influence the way we treat them, this, in turn, will affect the way they view themselves (their 'self concept') and their behaviour (Deluzain, 1996). This phenomenon is known as the 'self-fulfilling prophecy' and is one means by which stereotypes are quietly perpetuated in ways that we barely notice (Gross, 2005).

24

A classic research study by Gustav Jahoda (1954) reports an extreme practice of 'name stereotyping' amongst the Ashanti tribe of the Gold Coast, West Africa. Almost the entire Ashanti community believes that the day of the week on which a boy (but not a girl) is born affects both his personality and the way he will behave throughout his life. Boys born on a Monday are mild-mannered and peace-loving; those born on a Wednesday are violent and aggressive. So important is this influence that boys are given middle names indicating the day of their birth. On investigating the facts more closely, Jahoda found substantial evidence in support of the superstition. When he examined juvenile court records spanning a five-year period, he found that a far greater proportion of boys born on a Wednesday had been referred to the courts, and that these boys were responsible for 22 per cent of all the violent crimes recorded. Monday boys, by contrast, were far less likely than average to have court records, thus supporting the local superstition that they are peace-loving individuals. Jahoda concluded that the boys behaved exactly in accordance with the expectations of the community. Their names acted as a permanent reminder of their likely behaviour, reinforcing the self-fulfilling prophecy to the extent that it operated in an almost perfectly predictable way.

As you may have guessed, systematic stereotyping is not restricted to the Ashanti. Harari and McDavid (1973) explored the self-fulfilling prophecy effect among teachers in the USA. The researchers' aim was to find out the effects of students' names on teacher expectations. They did this by asking teachers to mark essays written by eleven-year-olds who were identified by their first names only. Essays by the students with 'attractive' names were marked as one grade higher than those by the students with 'unattractive' names. This effect was more marked for the boys' names (rank order: David, Michael, Elmer, Hubert) than for the girls' (rank order: Adele, Lisa, Karen, Bertha). Adele should have followed Lisa and Karen but the researchers point out that the name Adele has a strong scholarly stereotype that may have influenced the marking. When the essays were later marked again without the names they were all allocated similar grades.

Garwood (1976) set himself the task of finding out whether similar effects would be found among real pupils in a real school. He asked 79 teachers to rate boys' names as either 'desirable' or 'undesirable', then compared their scores for academic achievement. Garwood found that the average scores achieved by the group with desirable names were twice as high as those achieved by the unfortunate pupils with undesirable names. You will notice that this study looked into the stereotyping of boys only – and this leads me on to the point that a subtle difference exists between first-name stereotyping of boys and of girls. Busse and Seraydarian (1978) found that girls' popularity ratings in school were significantly related to the desirability of their first names. Boys' popularity with girls was also related to the popularity of their first names. However, when the effects of ethnicity and parental education were taken into account the popularity finding remained only for girls. West and Shults (1976) found that common male names were preferred to common female names but that uncommon male names were less popular than uncommon female names.

So much for name stereotyping in schools: the effect has been demonstrated in other settings too. Birmingham (2000) asked 464 consultant psychiatrists to diagnose a young person with mental health problems on the basis of a written case study alone. Four versions of the same document were sent out, the only difference being the names allocated: 'negative' names were Wayne and Tracey; 'positive' names were Matthew and Fiona. Matthew was diagnosed as schizophrenic more often than Wayne; however, Wayne was 18 per cent more likely than Matthew to be diagnosed as having a condition with pejorative connotations – such as a personality disorder, a substance-related disorder, or even 'feigning' or 'malingering'. This suggests that even psychiatrists, who are likely to be more aware than others of the dangers of labelling, cannot help being influenced by their stereotyped perception of particular names. There were no significant differences between Fiona and Tracey.

One fascinating piece of research relating to names was reported by Pelham *et al.* (2002), who suggest that we are all influenced by 'implicit egoism', which is an unconscious bias towards anything that might be associated with ourselves. Our own first name or surname may thus influence our choice of a place in which to settle (for example, people named Louis are especially likely to live in St Louis) and our choice of career (for example, people named Dennis and Denise are particularly likely to be dentists). We may even be more likely to marry someone whose surname or first name begins with the same letter as our own.

Given all that we have learnt about the importance of names it is worth pondering what the US parents of the 298 Armanis, 269 Chanels, 49 Canons and 353 girls named Lexus were thinking when they chose these names for their offspring in 2000. Is it all doom and gloom for children like these who have been given ridiculous names by their doting parents? No, Chanel, all is not lost. Psychologist Kenneth Steele reckons that many name stereotypes apply only in the absence of a photograph or

27

a face-to-face encounter. When he distributed lists of names that were 'desirable' (Jon, Joshua, Gregory) or 'undesirable' (Oswald, Myron, Reginald), the stereotypes held true. When he presented the names with photographs, the visual image erased any positive or negative impression created by the name alone (Steele and Smithwick, 1989).

Should you be saddled with a name that you believe is 'common' or otherwise undesirable, don't forget that an alternative form might create an altogether different impression. Leirer *et al.* (1982) found that people tend to associate different forms of common first names – such as the formal (Robert), familiar (Bob) and adolescent (Bobby) – with different personalities. You can also choose to use the separate parts of your name in different ways: Geoff Rolls (simple, informal, no frills, honest); Geoffrey William Rolls (more formal, serious, pretentious, not to be messed with); Geoff W Rolls (slightly ridiculous – and reminiscent of George W Bush); G W Rolls (mysterious, formal, gender hidden entirely); G Rolls (insignificant, dull, boring, gender still hidden).

So where does all this leave us? One thing is for sure: when the first Wayne, Shane, Sharon or Tracey arrives in Downing Street as Prime Minister we can be absolutely certain that he or she will have overcome a great deal of prejudice to get there – and will fully deserve the privileges that the position brings.

The creative
left-hander

There is a widely-
held belief that
left-handers are
not only a dab hand with
a paintbrush, tackling
activities that are more
artistic than the rest of
us would contemplate:
they may also possess

other special skills that make them much more creative than the
right-handed people who outnumber them by far. Julius Caesar,
Charlie Chaplin, Leonardo da Vinci, Albert Einstein, Paul
McCartney, John McEnroe, Brian Lara: all creative individuals
and all left-handed. Creativity is generally regarded as a useful
attribute and so it follows that this stereotype, unlike the vast
majority of others in this book, is positive.

At present, between seven and ten per cent of the adult
population are left-handed, making this a significant minority
group and one that may sometimes be neglected. More men are
left-handed than women (five men to every four women). Left-
handedness is also more common in identical twins (Hardyck
and Petrinovich, 1977), in homosexual men (Lalumière *et al.*, 2000)
and in people with neurological deficits such as autism, Down's
syndrome and epilepsy (Batheja and McManus, 1985).

There is now widespread acceptance of left-handedness but the
language that we use shows evidence of a lurking prejudice from
the past. The word 'sinister', which has negative connotations,
comes from the Latin word meaning 'left'; the word 'right' is a
positive word and a synonym for 'correctness' or 'accuracy' – it
also means 'an entitlement'. The adjective 'ambidextrous' is used

to describe a person who is able to use both hands with equal skill; however, the Latin word *dexter* means 'right' and the literal meaning of ambidextrous is therefore 'right-handed on both sides'. Coren (1992) suggests that the word 'footman' dates from a time when slaves or servants were positioned at the front door to ensure that guests entered a building with their right foot first.

Archaeological research indicates that left-handedness was about as prevalent in medieval times as it is now. During the industrial revolution of the 18th and 19th centuries an attempt was made to stamp it out completely, presumably to standardize the human interface with machines (Steele and Mays, 1995; McManus, 2002). Enforced right-handedness verged on the brutal: a child's left arm would be strapped to his or her side so that it could not be used and those children who strayed back to left-handedness were sometimes flogged. Cultural pressure persisted for many years, encouraging every young person to favour his or her right hand. As discrimination gradually reduced, the number of left-handers once more increased and continues to do so. It is believed that there are eight per cent more left-handers amongst 15- to 24-year-olds (eleven per cent) than amongst 55- to 64-year-olds (three per cent) (Raymond *et al.*, 1996).

Left-handed people are at considerable disadvantage in society because the vast majority of everyday tools are designed for right-handed people. Scissors and knives are the obvious examples but the computer mouse too was developed for the right-handed. Throughout the Western world, left-handers are unable to see their own handwriting, since it is hidden by the hand that is writing. (Left-handed writers of Arabic, Persian, Urdu or Hebrew do not have this problem, since these scripts run from right to left.) And before the invention of toilet paper – when the left hand was used for other purposes – things must have been a little tricky for them. Even the custom of shaking hands with the right hand displays a prejudice against the left-handed. In medieval times, shaking hands with your right hand meant that you wouldn't be able to draw your sword or knife (since these were carried in the right hand). Left-handed people couldn't be trusted because they would be perfectly capable of shaking hands with their right hand and plunging in a dagger with their left.

But it is not all bad news: left-handers enjoy considerable success in sport – and their prowess on the sports field may well have cheered on the positive stereotype. In football, the ideal team would have as many left-footed players as right; with only about ten per cent of the population being left-footed, players with this inbuilt advantage are rare – and much in demand. Many sportspeople are much more accustomed to playing against right-handed players. This is particularly evident in tennis, where right-handed players usually have difficulty in dealing with a left-hander's spin on the ball. The Spanish player Rafael Nadal is right-handed but was encouraged by his coach to play left-handed tennis, which the coach thought would be advantageous – and he has been proved right. Left-handed cricketers include two of the greatest West Indian batsmen, Garfield Sobers and Brian Lara. It's believed that having left-handers in the opposing team can disrupt a bowler's rhythm since he has to adjust his line accordingly. One of the greatest Indian batsmen, Sachin Tendulkar, bats with his right hand but writes with his left. To my knowledge there is just one sport in which it is definitely not advantageous to be left-handed: polo. The rules of this game dictate that holding a stick in your left hand is forbidden, which suggests extreme prejudice.

Now for a look at the science behind hand preference, which

will perhaps tell us more about the stereotype. Before considering this further, I will give you a quick summary of the structure of the brain, which is divided into two sides (hemispheres) and acts as a 'contra-lateral' control centre: this means that the right hemisphere of the brain controls the left side of the body and vice versa. The most obvious functions of the left hemisphere are the processing and control of speech and language – between 70 and 95 per cent of humans have left-hemisphere language specialization (Witelson and Pallie, 1973). The left hemisphere's other functions include logic and dealing with things in order. The right hemisphere's functions include emotional intuition and expression, spatial relations and the ability to deal with more than one thing at once.

It seems that a predisposition for hand preference is determined very early in life. An Oxford University team led by Clyde Francks has identified a gene (labelled LRRTM1) that influences left-handedness (Francks, Maegawa, Laurén *et al.*, 2007). Hand preference has been observed in the womb, where foetuses tend to suck the thumb on their preferred side (Hepper, McCartney and Shannon, 1998). The Geschwind theory (named after its originator, neurologist Norman Geschwind) suggests that higher rates of testosterone before birth make it more likely that a child will be left-handed. Testosterone suppresses the growth of the left hemisphere; as a result, the right hemisphere, which controls the left hand, is better prepared as the central processor of language although this is not its usual role (Salvesen *et al.*, 1993). Evidence to support this comes from Bragdon and Gamon (2004), who looked at the university degree choices of both right- and left-handers. They found that left-handers were far more likely to focus on visually-based as opposed to language-based subjects.

This may also explain the increased likelihood of a left-handed child developing dyslexia or speech disorders, which suggest right-hemisphere dominance.

Another theory suggests that left-handers and right-handers think in different ways – and the reasoning behind this may further endorse the creativity stereotype. Whereas right-handed people tend to solve problems one by one and in sequence (the linear sequential method), left-handed people tackle them in a simultaneous holistic way (the visual simultaneous method). As a result, left-handed people may be better at multitasking, which could be an important element of creativity. Waldfogel (2006) conducted research showing that left-handers earn slightly more than their right-handed cousins; perhaps the differences in the way they think may account for this discrepancy.

However, none of this is clear-cut. Being left-handed suggests that your right hemisphere may dominate, but this is by no means true in all cases. Being right-handed does not necessarily stop your right hemisphere from dominating. There is a considerable overlap between the abilities of right- and left-handers and the only certainty is that the relationship between left- and right-handedness and brain function is still not fully understood. The evidence seems to suggest that left-handed people may be more creative than right-handed people. However, there are far more right-handers in the population and therefore we are far more likely to come across creative right-handers than creative left-handers. Great partnerships can be formed between right- and left-handed people (Lennon and McCartney, for example) – as long as the left-hander knows what the right-hander is doing.

The dangerous stranger

The potential threat posed by strangers is something that we drum into our children at every opportunity. The stereotype that suggests that danger may lurk in deserted streets when we are out alone at night is now extended and  we must also warn our children that they can be in danger in broad daylight and in public places: never accept sweets from a stranger, never talk to a stranger, never get into a car with a stranger – and 'Run, yell and tell' if approached. Sadly, some high-profile murders of children have thrown a spotlight on the fact that a stranger may be dangerous. Toddler James Bulger was killed in 1993 by two ten-year-olds who abducted him when he was out shopping with his mother; Sarah Payne, aged eight, was murdered by a paedophile on a summer afternoon in 2000. In both these cases, the murderers were unknown to the victims. But in 2002, Holly Wells and Jessica Chapman, both aged ten, were murdered by their school caretaker Ian Huntley. Is our emphasis on 'stranger danger' justified, or is the danger lurking closer to home?

The perpetrators of real-life crimes against adults are rarely strangers – and most sexual crimes are committed by people who are known to their victims. A study by Lees (1996) found that only 14 per cent of reported rapes were committed by people unknown to their victims; 20 per cent had been raped by someone they had met within the 24 hours preceding the rape, 46 per cent by an acquaintance and 20 per cent by someone with whom they had previously had consensual sex. Rapes committed by known acquaintances are more likely to be under-reported than those committed by strangers. Koss *et al.* (1987) found that only two per cent of 'acquaintance rapes' were reported, in comparison to 21 per cent of 'stranger rapes'.

When it comes to crimes involving children, a similar pattern emerges. In a study of levels of child abuse, the National Society for the Prevention of Cruelty to Children (NSPCC) stated that five per cent of all children aged under 16 years report experiencing sexual abuse carried out by a stranger or someone they had just met; eleven per cent of children of the same age report sexual abuse by people known to them (Cawson *et al.*, 2000). The majority of the abuse involved family members, acquaintances or 'friends'. Similar statistics have been found in the USA: of the 93 per cent of child abuse cases where the children know their abusers, 40 per cent of the assaults occur in the victim's home and 20 per cent in the home of a friend, neighbour or relative (Bureau of Justice Statistics, 1997).

So why does the stranger danger myth exist at all, in the face of such substantial evidence to the contrary? Why is it that we are so preoccupied with the unlikely that we overlook the commonplace? One reason is that the media sometimes perpetuate the stereotype – and our gruesome fascination for the horrific may serve to encourage this. If we look closely, however, we often find that the fictional portrayal of even the most outrageously violent murderers suggests that they may, at times, seem 'normal' to their families and friends. Hannibal Lecter, played by Anthony Hopkins in *The Silence of the Lambs* (directed by Jonathan Demme, 1990), sometimes appears to be a civilized man with charm and intelligence, despite the fact that he is a serial killer. Other TV serials and movies that focus on the lives of people who commit appalling atrocities present us with similar ambiguities: for example, the US Emmy award-winning TV drama *Dexter* (2006), where Dexter Morgan is a serial killer who works for the Miami Police Department, and *American Psycho* (directed by Mary Harron, 2000).

Some newspapers like to label violent criminals as 'beasts' or 'animals', giving them special names such as the 'Yorkshire Ripper' or 'Boston Strangler' to emphasize how far removed they are from the rest of society (Soothill and Walby, 1991). Since we are understandably more comfortable with the idea of external evil than with the thought that it may be concealed within our midst (Baumeister, 1996), we are more than ready to believe that the perpetrators of violence are a race apart. However, this belief is dangerous: we assume that we would quickly spot a 'beast' or 'animal' when this is invariably not the case. One reason why some serial killers get away with their crimes for so long is precisely because of their 'ordinariness': communities cannot believe that they would be capable of performing such horrific crimes. The wife of the 'Yorkshire Ripper' Peter Sutcliffe, the lorry driver from Bradford who was convicted on 13 counts of murder and seven counts of attempted murder between 1976 and 1981, said that her husband was so 'normal' that she had never suspected him of such crimes. Many people could not believe that the good-looking, clean-cut law student Ted Bundy had killed 36 women during a four-year reign of terror in the USA during the 1970s. Even during his trial, in the face of overwhelming evidence of his guilt, people commented on his 'charming' demeanour.

Some feminist psychologists believe that our focus on the

'crazed killer' distracts us from the fact that violence is a 'normal' part of too many male–female relationships. Madriz (1997) suggests that an overemphasis on stranger danger helps to keep women 'in their place', constraining their lives and limiting their lifestyle choices – by discouraging them from going out alone at night, for example. In fact young men are far more at risk than women and women are far more likely to be harmed by people they know. In the UK, over 75 per cent of the victims of violent crime are male and men are twice more likely than women to be killed by strangers.

The risk of stranger danger is small, but is nonetheless a risk that none of us would want to underemphasize. It is surely better to be safe than sorry. Or is it? Barker (2008) suggests that one possible consequence of an overemphasis on stranger danger is the undermining of a true perspective of violence in our society. Not only are women made even more dependent on the male acquaintances who are most likely to be their aggressors; children too are restricted. Many children are no longer given the freedom of unsupervised outdoor play: instead they are closeted indoors, alone with their Nintendos®. An awareness of stranger danger has helped children to understand that strangers are potentially dangerous, but from this they may have deduced that non-strangers are harmless, which puts them at far greater risk. Paedophiles 'groom' children for precisely this reason: so that they are no longer seen as strangers. Whilst some of this grooming may take place on the internet, of the minority of cases perpetrated by those other than family members, friends or known acquaintances, only a small percentage involve the internet. The danger that our children may be abused by strangers whom they meet online may be another stereotype that the media has exaggerated.

We must be responsible in our attitude to risk, weighing up individually the possible dangers that we face and considering how best we can protect our offspring without restricting them unduly. A 'zero risk' approach will mean that our children don't go on school trips, play contact sports, walk to school or nip out to the corner shop. My belief is that such strict limits cannot be beneficial. The real risks lie much closer to home, which is a fact that should concern us all.

➡ *See also* The sadistic prison guard; The violent madman; The wicked stepmother.

The dirty old man

In the BBC TV comedy series *Steptoe and Son*, first screened in the 1960s, the character Harold Steptoe (pictured here with his TV father, Albert) was always criticizing his dad for being a 'dirty old man'. There is no doubt that dirty old men exist. Like Albert, they may be dirty in many senses, not least in their capacity for leering at a young woman. But is it possible to make a case for the defence of old chaps like these? In this discussion I want to explore briefly our evolutionary past and look at why it is that older men find it particularly difficult to ignore the lure of the younger woman.

It seems that we can make some excuses for the longings of older men, though whether they follow these through or not is their decision. It is hard-wired into our brains that reproduction is the key to our genes' survival and the more frequently a man has sex with a fertile woman, the greater the likelihood that he will have offspring. Nowadays, with the advent of the pill and other effective methods of contraception, sex is seen not only as the means of reproduction but also as a pleasurable activity in its own right. In the distant past, however, the evolutionary urge was paramount. Men are capable of fathering children and producing offspring at any age, the only obstacles being lack of energy and opportunity. In order to reproduce in their old age, men have to find themselves a mate who is younger – and in some cases, a great deal younger. This helps to explain why older men seek women who are still of child-bearing age, and are therefore increasingly younger than themselves.

Research suggests that women value men for the material resources that they can offer (Waynforth and Dunbar, 1995). With a lifetime of earnings behind them, plus any further funds they may have inherited from parents, older men may be very well equipped to offer financial security to a young wife and offspring. In this respect they can easily outdo their younger rivals, and this knowledge in itself may put extra lead in the old man's pencil.

It may sound simplistic to think of relationships in such black and white terms, but many women find attractive the financial security that an older man can offer. Some may even welcome the thought that, given the age difference, it may not be too many years 'til death does us part'. So next time you see an older man with a young and attractive woman, don't immediately think 'dirty old man'. He is simply succumbing to his evolutionary instincts – as, indeed, is she.

➡ *See also* The gold-digging woman and the looks-obsessed man; The sower of wild oats.

The dowdy librarian

Librarians in the movies always used to resemble the woman pictured here – female and bespectacled. They were also dowdy, introverted, unmarried, timid, prim and shy. In the film *It's a Wonderful Life*, directed by Frank Capra (1946) and starring Jimmy Stewart and Donna Reed, Jimmy Stewart's character, George Bailey, realizes that the loss of a bank deposit will ruin his buildings and loan business – and he contemplates suicide. However, God sends an angel who shows him what might have happened to his loved ones if he'd never been born. His wife, played by Donna Reed, has become a spinster librarian and is seen emerging from the library in a dowdy, unflattering outfit, wearing glasses and no make-up. This and other such episodes persuade Stewart not to jump – but to face the future and turn his life around. In his case, seeing his wife as a librarian was literally a fate worse than death.

The *Radio Times* voted *It's a Wonderful Life* as the second-best film never to have won an Oscar®. Right at the top of the list was the much more recent movie *The Shawshank Redemption* (1994), directed by Frank Darabont – in which the main protagonist and hero, Andy Dufresne (played by Tim Robbins), is a prisoner librarian who presents a very positive image for the profession: he gives his fellow inmates hope for the future through their work in the prison library. This and many other films since the 1970s have provided a variety of refreshing and original portrayals of librarians – witness Goldie Hawn in *Foul Play* (directed by Colin Higgins, 1978) as a librarian who discovers a plot to kill the Pope, and Parker Posey's free-spirited young librarian Mary in the 1995 romantic comedy *Party Girl*, directed by Daisy von Scherler Mayer.

Walker and Lawson (1993) argue that Hollywood's portrayal of librarians does not influence the public's view of them quite as much as we might expect. However, whatever the influences, members of this undervalued profession are dogged by pervasive negative stereotypes. Perhaps one of the reasons for this is that most librarians are female: people who work in many of the professions that are staffed largely by women – such as secretarial work and nursing – are vulnerable to stereotyping and are sometimes held in low esteem. (Air stewardesses once fell into the same category, but as 'flight attendants' they are slightly less prone to this treatment.) Many men who choose these professions are also negatively stereotyped (Carmichael, 1992). Kirkendall (1986) claims that members of the public describe librarians in general as quiet, stern, unmarried, stuffy and wearing glasses.

Green (2005) believed that the stereotypical librarian is an older woman, single, with grey hair that she wears in a bun; she is tall and thin, with a pallid complexion. Following a fun survey of all librarians in the New South Wales region of Australia, he was able to draw a much more accurate picture. He concluded that, as expected, a real librarian is likely to be a woman – 82 per cent of the librarians surveyed were female – and she probably wears glasses (84 per cent do). But there the stereotype ends. The typical librarian is in a long-term relationship (like 84 per cent of the respondents) and aged around 48 years. Librarians describe themselves as fun, serious, eccentric, extroverted, cheerful, optimistic, jolly, friendly, obnoxious, life and soul of the party, warm, welcoming, energetic, friendly and outgoing – not dissimilar to the typical Australian then … As per the stereotype, the average librarian has a fair complexion (74 per cent) – although, not surprisingly, she does not describe herself as 'pallid'. She has short hair (69 per cent) that is brown or black in colour (50 per cent): please note that only 21 per cent of librarians fit the grey-hair stereotype. 'Tall and thin' goes the stereotype, but this body shape was definitely in the minority among those surveyed. And the most surprising fact of all? Eleven per cent of the librarians in Green's survey had tattoos.

You only have to visit your local library to know that very few librarians fit the stereotyped image. Many are extremely upset by the negative stereotypes associated with their profession, and some believe that too much time and energy is wasted on discussing them (Paul and Evans, 1988). *The Image of the Library: Studies and Views from Several Countries* (Stelmakh, 1994) includes this statement from Australian author John Frylinck:

> Most of us use stereotyping of some sort everyday. Faced with a complex set of information about people or occupations, the tendency is to simplify these facts by extracting only the most obvious. Although other careers have stereotypes, librarians seem to take alleged misrepresentations of their image more seriously than others.
>
> Stelmakh, 1994

Cheer up librarians, it may be that the public perception of you is not as negative as you may think. A 1988 study suggests that college students give librarians a positive rating, concluding that they should leave their worries behind and instead channel their energies into informing the public about the wide variety of services that they provide (Morrizey and Case, 1988). They are a lively bunch: after all, Batgirl was a librarian; Casanova, the world's greatest lover, gave up womanizing to become a librarian. (Perhaps he should have destroyed the stereotype once and for all by keeping up both interests simultaneously.) And there are numerous websites and blogs written by librarians that appear to break the librarian stereotype – just take a look at the Belly Dancing Librarian and the Lipstick Librarian.

One final nugget of information for you. In the interests of research I have investigated the librarian fantasies that many men indulge in, and this is how they go: the dowdy librarian removes her glasses, shakes the pins from her hair and is instantly transformed into a sexy nymphette with a hint of dominatrix. If this wish were to come true I am sure that poor standards of literacy amongst adolescent boys would quickly become a thing of the past.

The dumb blonde

A husband and his blonde wife are woken by a phone call at three in the morning. The blonde picks up the phone, listens to the caller and replies, 'How the hell should I know, it's 200 miles from here!' When her husband asks, 'Who was that?' she responds, 'I don't know. Someone who wanted to know if the coast is clear!'

This joke, and thousands more, exploit the 'dumb blonde' stereotype, which is most frequently applied to blonde women who, although popular and attractive, are considered to lack both intelligence and common sense. Some blondes – scientist Susan Greenfield and politicians Margaret Thatcher and Hillary Clinton are all blondes at the time of writing – call the stereotype seriously into question. We could debate at length the extent of their cleverness (as well as the authenticity of their hair colour), but the dumb blonde stereotype persists nonetheless.

It must be obvious to everyone (even blondes) that the stereotype has little or no grounding in fact – and neither is it supported by research. So how did it evolve? Some claim that the epithet 'dumb blonde' may have been coined to describe Rosalie Duthé, an 18th-century Parisian prostitute who was famous for her long silences – appearing dumb in the most literal sense. In 1775, Rosalie Duthé became the subject of a one-act play, *Les Curiosités de la Foire*, which Paris audiences found hilarious. Others claim that it was the 1925 novel *Gentlemen Prefer Blondes*, by US author and screenwriter Anita Loos, that created the stereotype; Marilyn Monroe starred in the 1953 film of the same title. Though not a natural blonde, Monroe excelled in the 'dumb blonde' role in this and many other movies. Meanwhile some academics reject both these dumb blonde prototypes in favour of a much simpler explanation. Many Caucasian babies have blond hair that darkens with age: thus blond hair is associated with childishness and, by implication, inexperience and limited understanding.

In the West, men regard women with blond hair as attractive. Kanazawa and Kovar (2004) argue that, when seeking a partner, men go for looks and women for resources (such as income and status). As intelligent men generally have a higher income and status than stupid men, good-looking blondes are more likely to end up with clever and wealthy male partners. Since blondness can be influenced by heredity (though it is a recessive trait), and intelligence is the fruit of both nature and nurture, the children of such unions may be both intelligent and blond. There may therefore be a correlation, if only a weak one, between intelligence and blondness in both men and women. So why do we cling to the dumb blonde stereotype? Perhaps because even blonde women have been able to work out what men want the most – and that's not usually a wife with a degree. Therefore blondes may well invest their energies in snagging a wealthy, high-status man rather than in their own education. This is not evidence of stupidity: they're just targeting their resources appropriately (Frank, 2007).

Blondes are certainly not dumb. Amongst the more believable speculations that surround Marilyn Monroe is the rumour that she had an intelligence quotient (IQ) of 160 or more. Nevertheless, many people, both men and women, still regard the stereotype as gospel. Cassidy and Harris (1999) asked 60 men and 60 women to look at pictures of a female model wearing in turn four differently coloured wigs: platinum blonde, natural blonde, brown and red. Participants were asked to rate the model for intelligence, shyness, aggression, temperament and popularity. The platinum blonde model was rated as less intelligent, particularly by men, the brown-haired model was rated as more shy and the natural blonde as more popular. So it seems that the 'dumb' stereotype may be focused particularly on platinum blondes.

A word of caution if you are allowing yourself to entertain for a few moments the possibility that blondes may really be dumb: merely being aware of a stereotype can affect your behaviour, and you could find the 'blonde effect' rubbing off on you. Bargh *et al.* (1996) have shown that when people are in the company of an elderly person they tend to walk and talk more slowly. Similarly, our performance in a general knowledge test can be affected by those around us: people taking the test in the company of a top model do not perform as well as those taking it with university professors, whom they associate with intelligence (Dijksterhuis and van Knippenberg, 1998).

It seems that some of us are more susceptible than others to such influences. Bry *et al.* (in press) found that some people show a strong tendency to be 'connected, related or integrated with others', and these they identified as having 'interdependent personalities'. The researchers showed men and women 20 faces of either blonde women or brown-haired men and the participants had to describe the hair colour shown; a control group saw no faces at all. Afterwards, all participants took a multiple-choice general knowledge test. Of those who had been shown the blondes, both men and women who were previously rated as having 'interdependent personalities' performed less well than the participants who had viewed the faces with brown hair and the members of the control group. The conclusion was that the 'blonde effect' exerts a real and measurable influence on some people.

So although there is ample scientific proof that blondes are not dumb, people still seem to believe that the stereotype is true – for the platinum blonde in particular. Pitman (2003) argues that the 'dumb blonde' stereotype is a device used by men and by brunettes who feel threatened, giving them an opportunity to debase and devalue the power of blonde women. If this is true, the jokes are set to continue. Perhaps it's true that brunettes are so jealous that they sit around making up jokes about blondes. I wonder if they know this one:

Question: Why are blonde jokes so short?
Answer: So brunettes can remember them.

➡ *See also* The gentleman who prefers blondes; The gold-digging woman and the looks-obsessed man; The passionate redhead.

The emotional woman

The stereotype that women are more emotional than men is widespread and ancient. The word for an extreme show of emotion, 'hysteria', comes from the Greek word *hysterā* (meaning 'womb') and hysteria is by definition a uniquely female condition. When asked about the qualities of another person, 90 per cent of people apply the characteristic 'emotional' more frequently to women than to men.

In babyhood, boys and girls cry approximately the same amount, but by puberty, girls cry more than boys; by the age of 18, they cry four times more than boys (Witchalls, 2003). One possible explanation for women's tearfulness may lie in the fact that they have more of the hormone prolactin, which is present in tears. It is also the case that women's tear ducts are shaped differently from men's, although whether this is the cause or the effect of more crying is unknown. The higher incidence of depression among women – some even suggest that this is because of the way men treat them – would certainly explain the fact that they cry more frequently.

Although there may be a biological explanation for females' heightened emotions, this does not take effect until puberty. Perhaps this can be explained by the fact that, in the West, we typically encourage boys to be strong and tough and girls to be nurturing and caring. In this respect, emotional women may be the product of our gender-specific expectations. A person whose behaviour is inconsistent with the gender stereotype (a crying man or a dominant woman, for example) may attract more attention and be regarded as more genuine than a person who conforms. Whilst a crying woman is dismissed as 'just another emotional woman' who is 'overreacting', a crying man is a rare and honest creature who has the courage to show his feelings, and whose distress may be taken more seriously. Or at least that *was* the case until 1990, when footballer Paul Gascoigne shed copious tears at the World Cup in Italy, thus setting the trend for men to cry in public.

Ron Levant, a professor at Harvard University, suggests that men in the West undergo a socialization process that hampers their emotional development. Women possess a range of emotional responses that enable them to understand others' perspectives and emotions and thereby develop 'emotional empathy'. Men, with their strong emphasis on 'doing' and 'fixing the problem', have only 'action empathy' at their disposal. Levant also claims that most men have only two responses to emotional issues: issues associated with vulnerability (fear or shame, for example) are dealt with using anger; issues associated with nurturing (loving or intimacy, for example) are dealt with through sex. The 'traditional male stereotype' so prevalent in the West encourages these responses: the Marlboro® man, male film stars, sportsmen, competitive dads … all these promote a stereotype of what it means to be a 'real man', and any boy who deviates from it risks ridicule, teasing and isolation from his peers (Levant, 1997).

One reason why women may be seen as more emotional than men relates to the way in which their memories work. Women have generally been found to have superior memories for emotionally significant events: for example, they recall more quickly, more vividly and with more emotional intensity than their spouses any memories concerning their first date, last holiday or most recent argument (Fujita *et al.*, 1991). There are two possible explanations for this. The first is the 'affect–intensity' hypothesis, which suggests that women encode these memories better than men because they experience life more intensely. The second is the 'cognitive style' hypothesis, which suggests that women are more likely than men to encode, rehearse and think about the emotions associated with the experience – and this helps to enhance and consolidate the memory.

Canli *et al.* (2002) asked twelve men and twelve women to study 96 pictures of varying emotional significance: these ranged from an emotion-free book cover to an emotion-laden picture of a dead person. Three weeks later, when all participants were asked to recall the images, women were 15 per cent more successful than men at remembering the emotional images. During their recall of the images, all the participants underwent brain scans. These showed that the two areas of the brain used separately for emotional processing and memory formation seem to overlap more in women than in men. This may indicate a biological cause for women's better recall of emotional events; however it is equally possible that the difference in the 'wiring' of the brain has developed as a response to cultural socialization processes and is thus a result rather than a cause. It is nevertheless interesting that scientific evidence now supports the assertion that women tend to dwell more than men on emotional memories – a fact that women have been aware of for many years.

It may well be that women are regarded as emotional because of physiological changes that affect their emotions at particular times in their menstrual cycle. Many a man has secretly wondered whether the tongue-lashing he has just received can be blamed on the 'time of the month'. Pre-menstrual syndrome (PMS) or pre-menstrual tension (PMT) is experienced by 90 per cent of women; about 30 per cent find that it has a significant negative effect and for between five and ten per cent this effect is severe. Over 100 symptoms are associated with PMS and the most common of these specifically affect the emotions, causing irritability, mood swings, depression and unexplained tearfulness (Owen, 2005). However, PMS is an extremely controversial topic. Some feminist academics emphasize the fact that normal functioning should never be labelled a 'disorder', pointing out that PMS has only been viewed as such since the time when women entered the workforce in larger numbers. They also suggest that PMS is used by men as a method of 'social control', enabling them to subjugate and stereotype women as 'the weaker sex'.

In some societies, menstruation is regarded more positively than it is in most Western cultures. As for PMS, neither the diagnosis nor the definition of this condition is universal and it is primarily a Western creation: whilst other cultures recognize that women are affected by their cycle they do not find it necessary to classify these effects as a syndrome. Psychologists are divided in their views concerning the PMS label. Feminist psychologists such as Caplan (1995) believe that it leads to unnecessary stigmatizing of women, with the implication that they become mentally 'out of control' once a month; other psychologists believe that it helps all of us to understand the potential severity of the symptoms.

A surprising study reported by Aubeeluck at a British Psychological Society (BPS) conference in 2004 (BPS, 2004) claims that men also suffer from monthly mood swings. Aubeeluck asked 50 men and 50 women to complete a questionnaire assessing a range of symptoms usually related to the menstrual cycle. Men reported at least as many of the symptoms as women, but attributed the effects to other causes. Aubeeluck suggested that two possible conclusions may be drawn from this: women do not suffer from PMS and/or men too may suffer from cyclical monthly changes, as yet undiagnosed. A third conclusion might be that the men's symptoms arise in response to their partners' PMT behaviours.

In conclusion, it is clear that, for whatever reason, women are more likely than men to show their feelings. However, men can be brought up to show their feelings more and to be more emotionally aware; in fact, emotional intelligence may soon be regarded as a prerequisite for a successful life. No longer is it appropriate for a man simply to leave home and go out hunting for food; nowadays it is essential that he can work cooperatively in a team, listen to other people's views and relate emotionally to work colleagues – as well as interacting effectively with his partner and their children.

The faithful hound

I have a lovely collie-cross Labrador called Maisie, adored by the whole family. When she nearly died through indulging in a bit of unsupervised chocolate, I felt as though my heart was breaking – and it wasn't just because of the vet's bill. On the other hand, dogs occasionally attack and kill people, often smell, playfully knock over young children and (somewhat embarrassingly) try to hump your aged aunt's leg on Christmas Day. Some say that a dog is a man's best friend. But surely, these are hardly the kinds of behaviour that one would expect from a buddy?

Actually we know very well why dogs are so highly revered: for the most part they are affectionate, intelligent and loyal to the point of devotion. What's more, research shows that people who have dogs as pets are generally healthier and happier than those who don't. Many find that dog-walking provides a pleasant interlude from the stresses and strains of life and also increases social interaction. What could be more relaxing than pounding along a sandy beach with your faithful hound – or simply allowing him or her to drag you around the block. Dogs also provide unconditional love and increase emotional wellbeing; in addition, they can help people to recover from bereavement. Dog owners have even been shown to have more robust immune systems. I hear some of you asking whether other pets can bestow all these blessings on their owners ... The answer is probably not. Although some cat lovers claim that cats are better to have around the house than dogs, there is no evidence to support this – possibly because, with all those walks, dog owners are more active and less overweight than cat owners.

It is unclear where the expression 'man's best friend' originated, although many attribute it to Senator George Graham Vest of Missouri (1830–1904). Before entering Congress, Vest was a noted lawyer. (In those days, politicians had useful careers before they entered politics.) In a court case concerning a man who had shot someone's dog, Vest gave a famous 'Eulogy on the Dog' summing-up speech, in which he said:

> The one absolutely unselfish friend that man can have in this selfish world, the one that never deserts him, the one that never proves ungrateful or treacherous, is his dog.
>
> *Congressional Record*, 1914

Over time, these words were reduced and crystallized into the neat expression that is so frequently used today: a dog is a man's best friend. And so it is that the 'faithful hound' stereotype came into being.

The saying is, of course, applicable to both men and women. Actually, dogs seem to be even more highly regarded by women than by men. A survey in the USA found that 56 per cent of the women surveyed (compared to 41 per cent of the men) found their pets more affectionate than their partners; 45 per cent of the women (compared to 24 per cent of the men) found their pets cuter than their partners. More women than men reported that they had a deep emotional connection with their pets. Nearly all women respondents (99 per cent, compared with 95 per cent of men) reported that they frequently talked to their pets (Bizrate Survey,

....

2005). These surprising results suggest that a dog is actually a *woman's* best friend.

Now let's investigate some more of the research and see what objective evidence it provides concerning the special relationship between dogs and humans. Without a shadow of doubt, the research reinforces our hunch that dogs are good for us. Research reported in 2005 at the American Heart Association's Scientific Sessions (described by Laino, 2005) showed that a twelve-minute hospital visit by a trained volunteer with a dog had clear and positive benefits for the patient. The experiment involved a specially-trained dog (from one of twelve different breeds) lying on a patient's bed so that the patient could touch the animal while interacting with the volunteer-plus-dog team. Researchers monitoring the physical indicators of patients' anxiety (such as blood pressure, heart function and resistance of the blood vessels) found that anxiety scores dropped 24 per cent as a result of the visits. Scores for the volunteer-only group dropped by just ten per cent and the at-rest group's score did not change at all. Levels of the stress hormone adrenaline dropped by an average of 17 per cent in the volunteer-plus-dog group and two per cent in the volunteer-only group, whereas they rose by an average of seven per cent in the at-rest group. All the monitoring demonstrated that patients showed most improvement when a dog was involved in the interaction.

These findings are further reinforced by Banks (2006), who found that nursing home residents felt far less lonely after spending time alone with a dog than they did when they were visited by a dog accompanied by other people. It was also found that the loneliest people benefited the most from the dogs' visits. Of course, dogs can also play a more direct therapeutic role

– by helping visually impaired, hearing impaired and disabled people, for example. They are also used by the police, by airport security and as sniffer dogs to detect drugs. Some breeds, such as the St Bernard, are specially trained as search and rescue dogs: with their superior sense of smell they are more successful than humans at finding people who have been trapped following an earthquake, avalanche or bomb blast.

But dogs don't just give assistance with problems or emergencies: some, such as guard dogs, gun dogs and sled dogs, play an important part in our everyday working lives. Dogs also help us by taking an active part in scientific research. In fact, dogs took part in one of the most famous studies ever, which explored how organisms learn. While studying the digestive system of dogs, the Russian physiologist Ivan Pavlov (1849–1936) noticed that his laboratory dogs had learned to salivate at the sound of the footsteps of the man who came to feed them (Pavlov, 1927). This learning process, which Pavlov called 'classical conditioning' or 'learning by association', also occurs in humans – that's why the mere sight of an advert for a particular brand of drink may well make you feel thirsty.

Why else might dogs be our best friends? As dogs and man have been coexisting for at least 15,000 years, the answer may lie in the long-standing relationship between the two species. During this time, humans have selectively bred in dogs those traits that they wished to encourage: the dogs that worked the hardest, or were the most sociable, were used for breeding – and this led to the most useful traits remaining and prospering in the dog gene pool. Furthermore, a remarkable 94 per cent of a dog's genetic sequence is the same as ours (Biello, 2005).

Chimps are even more closely related to us genetically, and

wolves have bigger brains than dogs. So we would not necessarily expect dogs' communication skills to come out tops. Nevertheless, researchers examining the abilities of wolves, chimpanzees and domesticated dogs found that the dogs, even those as young as nine weeks old, were the most skilled in following human instructions on the location of hidden food.

It is likely that evolutionary 'selection' played an important part in encouraging dogs to develop the characteristics that humans particularly appreciate in them – including the ability to understand and follow instructions. Evolutionary selection is defined in *The Chambers Dictionary* as 'the process by which some individuals contribute more offspring than others to the next generation' (Chambers, 2008). Many of our likes and dislikes have clearly been shaped by evolutionary selection. For example, we perceive sugar as sweet because those ancestors who consumed sweet fruits derived energy and nutrition from them and thrived; those who did not died out. This study suggests that the influence of natural selection on the coevolution of dogs with humans favoured a set of cognitive abilities – thinking skills – that make the bond between humans and dogs unique (Walton, 2002).

The special human–canine relationship is demonstrated in numerous situations, some of which have involved children being looked after by dogs. In 2005, a newborn baby girl was wrapped in a plastic bag and abandoned in the Lenana forest on the outskirts of Nairobi, Kenya, where she lay undiscovered for two days. Then someone reported the unusual sight of a dog carrying a baby in its mouth. At last the police found the child – nestled snugly amongst a pile of puppies that the dog had given birth to a few days previously. The dog had tried to care for her as best she could. The baby was taken to the local hospital and made a full recovery from her unusual experience (Reagan, 2005). Even more remarkable is the story of six-year-old Ivan Mishukov, who left his mother and her alcoholic boyfriend to fend for himself on the streets of Reutova, west of Moscow, in the 1980s. Ivan earned the trust of a pack of wild dogs by stealing food for them, and spent two years living with the pack in an extremely inhospitable climate – where winter temperatures plummet to –30°C. When the police tried to 'rescue' the boy, the dogs defended him; eventually a bait trap was laid for them at a local restaurant. Ivan was taken into care and later resumed normal schooling (Newton, 2002). Both of these examples, along with many others, surely demonstrate the unique regard that man has for dogs and vice versa.

Of course, there is a limit to a dog's understanding, so let's not get too carried away here. Some owners have claimed to have psychic pets who, when left at home, can sense their imminent return. In 1994, one owner making such a claim allowed her dog to be filmed for British TV. This attracted a fair amount of interest until some spoilsport psychologists put the claims to the test. Four carefully-controlled experiments revealed that Jaytee, the dog in question, didn't have a clue as to when his owner would come home (Wiseman *et al.*, 1998).

I'm almost convinced about a dog being a man's best friend. However, dogs do have one irritating habit that can sometimes prove fatal to their faithful owners. A dog will occasionally take a stroll across a frozen pond and then fall through the ice. The owner invariably dies trying to save the dog, who scrambles out, unharmed, further along the bank.

When a faithful hound does, finally, come to the end of its life, we dog owners again demonstrate our high regard for our furry companions. People sometimes respond to the death of a dog in much the same way as they do to the death of a family member (Morey, 2006). We are more likely to bury a dog than any other animal, and there is evidence that we have done so for between 12,000 and 14,000 years. Such practices provide yet more evidence of the strong relationship between the two species – if a dog is a man's best friend, that friendship is certainly reciprocated.

The football hooligan

Professional football is the most popular spectator sport in England (Williams, 2001). Unfortunately for the vast majority of peaceful football fans, many England supporters are stereotyped as hooligans, only too eager to take on anyone who wants a fight. Although records of football hooliganism date back to the nineteenth century, this phenomenon came to the fore both in the media and in the minds of the public in the 1960s. Sadly, it entered a new realm of magnitude in 1985 when Liverpool fans charged on Juventus supporters at Heysel Stadium in Brussels – and 39 people died as a result of a wall collapsing. After this, all English teams were banned from European competitions for five years.

Football hooliganism is often termed the 'English disease'. Many other countries, notably Germany, Holland, Turkey, Italy and France, also suffer from spectator violence at football matches. Nevertheless, the English football supporter is seen as the living embodiment of hooliganism for three reasons: because of the long history of hooliganism in England, because football hooliganism has been exported to Europe when English teams play abroad and because spectator violence is now associated with the English national team (Dunning *et al.*, 1988). As a result, the trappings of the England supporter, such as the cross of St George (pictured here) or the Football Association shirt, are slowly becoming associated with disruption and violence.

Social scientists have been studying crowd behaviour in both sporting and non-sporting contexts for over 100 years, and there are various psychological theories that seek to explain it. One of the earliest theorists was Gustave Le Bon (1895) who wrote that 'an individual in a crowd descends several rungs of the ladder of civilisation'. He suggested that individuals may suffer from a sense of anonymity (later termed de-individuation) in the crowd situation and thus become less aware of their own actions. This lack of responsibility or accountability makes violent behaviour more likely. A 'collective mindset' takes over and the crowd acts as one. This 'contagion' theory suggests that crowds make people behave in particular ways.

One problem with this theory is that the de-individuation experienced in a crowd situation does not always lead to antisocial behaviour. Witness the peaceful behaviour of large crowds that regularly gather for music festivals, or the mass of quiet onlookers who lined the route for Princess Diana's funeral procession in 1997. An alternative and more modern view of crowd behaviour involves 'convergent' theory. This theory suggests that like-minded individuals converge to behave in like-minded ways. In the case of football hooliganism, it is not the crowd dynamics but the fans' pre-existing feelings of hatred that cause the violence. Put simply, violent people are attracted to football because it provides a ready outlet for their violence. Perhaps this and the 'de-individuation' effect combine, heightening the violence.

Another theory concerning crowd behaviour is the snappily entitled 'emergent-norm theory of crowd dynamics' proposed by Turner and Killian (1972). Turner and Killian suggest that crowd behaviour is neither irrational nor entirely predictable. Their view is that groups of similar people often gather in crowds for some collective purpose (to cheer on their team, for example), but that the purpose may change during the course of the event. Specific factors may alter the norms within the crowd: in the case of football, these factors might include the result, a referee's decision or the way in which the crowd is policed. Individuals within the crowd may arrive at the stadium looking forward to a joyous celebration of victory; during the day, however, unexpected and less fortuitous events may have an adverse effect on their behaviour.

Stott and Adang (2003) give some possible reasons for the fact that football is more prone to hooliganism than other sports. The dynamics of a crowd are a mixture of internal and external crowd influences and the 'social identity' theory suggests that a crowd's collective behaviour is influenced by the shared identity of its members. In the case of football supporters, the sense of identity will include their loyalty to a particular team and their feelings for the opposition. It will also include anything else that they believe they share: for example, shared history or experiences and possibly a white, macho, working-class background, if you will excuse the stereotype. Specific aspects of social identity may unite a crowd even if these aspects are irrelevant to the situation in which they find themselves: for example, Scottish football fans often unite around their negative feelings towards the English, even when Scotland are not playing England.

Although crowd behaviour is affected by this sense of social identity, research suggests that the behaviour of a crowd is also determined by how the two sets of fans interact during the match and how each group believes that it has been treated during the event. Stott and Adang (2003) emphasize the role played by local officials in controlling football crowds; they suggest that the police in particular can strongly influence crowd behaviour, ensuring that the likelihood of violence is minimal. If football supporters are treated as mindless thugs, then they may well behave as such.

Armstrong (1994, 1998) is of the view that violence is an attractive option for many football supporters because it gives them a 'sense of belonging'. In what Armstrong sees as a form of 'social drama', fans may believe that inflicting shame on rival groups of supporters is a way of acquiring honour for themselves. In similar vein, Gerry Finn (1994) sees hooliganism as a means by which individuals may experience emotional peaks that are missing from other areas of their lives. In this respect there may be parallels between football hooliganism and other risk-taking activities – for example, joyriding.

A common explanation for football hooliganism places the blame on the consumption of alcohol. Although this plays a part in some incidents, widespread drinking also occurs at many other sporting events, such as rugby and cricket, where hooliganism is extremely rare. Moreover, drink is often restricted at and around many football stadia. The supporters of certain teams (Denmark, for example) are renowned for their alcohol intake at matches yet they are also known to be among the least violent football fans of recent years.

The explanations for football hooliganism are varied, complex and only partially understood. Although some suggest that the violence may be ritualistic (Marsh *et al.*, 1978), pre-planned and deliberately organized by ringleaders, the fact remains that the hooligans themselves are often unsure as to why it happens. Given the high level of football spectatorship in this country, and the fact that most spectators are loyal to one particular side, there is always the chance that a small minority of spectators will act violently in any contest. Nevertheless, the vast majority of football fans display great rivalry in a non-violent and often friendly or humorous way. Football hooliganism is certainly not restricted to the English, and our growing understanding of the phenomenon suggests that it often involves young men of any nationality acting in predictable ways. All the same, it is difficult to get away from the idea that individuals who are set on causing trouble find that the 'tribal' attitudes of football supporters make for an atmosphere that is conducive to violence. When England fail to qualify for a major championship, and a dark cloud hangs over the country as a result, the silver lining is that its supporters will not, this time, bring the country into disrepute.

The funny clown

Clowns have existed for thousands of years, throughout history and in most cultures: one of the earliest known references to a performing clown dates from Egypt's Fifth Dynasty – around 2500 BC. Nowadays we expect little more of a clown than slapstick humour. In the past, however, a clown was a wise social commentator and sometimes the only person given the right to question or reflect upon a ruler's decisions. Several of Shakespeare's plays (*King Lear*, for example) show clearly that the court jester or 'fool' was able to subvert convention to reveal moral truths, often making shrewd and influential observations on affairs of state. Satirical TV might be seen as today's equivalent to the grand clowning tradition, although whether our leaders pay any attention to it is another matter.

The appearance of the modern clown figure dates back to Joseph Grimaldi (1778–1837), who was the first to sport the now-stereotypical white face, exaggerated smile and red nose. So successful was this founding father of clowning as we know it that the name 'Joey' is sometimes used as a nickname for clowns today. No longer regarded as a source of wisdom, the primary purpose of most present-day clowns is to entertain. The stereotype is that clowns make us laugh and are hilariously funny. But is this really how people perceive them?

The answer is no. Strangely, clowns are stereotyped in a dichotomous way, as either very funny or very scary. A clown's appearance exaggerates certain human features – not only facial features are exaggerated but also other body parts, such as the feet and hands, which may become huge. Although these exaggerations are meant to be humorous, they may also be seen as monstrous deformities. My friend Lloyd detests clowns with a passion and it seems he's not alone. Clown phobia is suffered by as many as eight per cent of all phobics and has even been given a name: coulrophobia. Even if they are not coulrophobic, many adults find clowns repulsive – not least the intruder who shot dead two clowns in the midst of a circus performance in the eastern Colombian city of Cúcuta in 2007. At first the audience thought this was part of the act, only later realizing that it was no laughing matter (BBC News, 2007).

Hollywood has helped to promote the 'clowns are frightening' idea in numerous horror films where clowns have committed all sorts of atrocities. Setting aside the clown named the Joker in the not-too-frightening Batman films, perhaps the best-known example of a truly terrifying clown is Stephen King's Pennywise. In the spine-chilling film *It*, which is based on King's 1986 novel of the same title and was directed by Tommy Lee Wallace (1990), Pennywise abducts children in order to feed on them in the sewer. Bart Simpson has got in on the act, too, when he reports that he can't fall asleep because he is worried that the clown will eat him in the animated US TV show *The Simpsons*.

Research has revealed that children in particular find clowns both strange and scary. A Sheffield University research team, headed by Penny Curtis, showed pictures of clowns to 250 children aged between four and sixteen years. The team found 'that clowns are universally disliked by children. Some found them quite frightening and unknowable.' Psychologist Patricia Doorbar agrees, stating that 'Very few children like clowns. They are unfamiliar and come from a different era. They don't look funny, they just look odd' (BBC News, 2008).

Some psychologists have suggested that the fear of clowns may develop at an early age, when infants first begin to process and understand facial features. A clown's constant inane grin does not change to fit the circumstances and it is easy to imagine that this might be frightening to a young child who does not know how to interpret it (Rohrer, 2008). This childhood fear may be so pronounced that it carries on into adulthood – particularly if perpetuated by the occasional horror film. In fact some have attributed the fear of clowns as being specifically due to adolescents watching the film *It* when they were at a particularly vulnerable and impressionable age.

Given the fact that many children find clowns macabre and sinister, it is surprising that they are frequently employed in hospitals to 'cheer up' the youngest patients. Svebak (2006) examined the link between humour, stress and mortality rates. Although he cheerfully concluded that humour has positive benefits and can be 'crisis-minimizing', he is less than convinced by the idea of sending in the clowns. People respond to humour by means of various different processes, including the cognitive (the ability to understand humour), the social (the ability to get along with people who are funny) and the affective (one's predilection for smiling and laughing). Sveback suggests that interaction with a clown is likely to operate on the affective level only – and will not, therefore, be as effective as it might. There is also a risk that children will simply not be amused by a peculiar person with a large red nose. Of course, many hospital clowns are well aware that some children find them scary and try to adapt their behaviour accordingly. But perhaps it is time we all took

heed of the fact that the term 'clowning around' is usually used
only when someone is being annoying and stupid rather than
funny.

The gentleman who prefers blondes

Research suggests that men concentrate on physical attractiveness when they seek a potential partner. One way in which psychologists have attempted to find out whether men really prefer blondes is to analyse the depiction of women in magazines. Rich and Cash (1993) categorized the hair colour of cover models for *Vogue, Ladies' Home Journal* and *Playboy* magazine from the 1950s to the 1980s. (It's a tough job, but someone has to do it.) The

researchers then compared the frequency of blondes appearing on the covers of each of these magazines to the proportion of blondes in the Caucasian population. Results revealed that blondes appeared more frequently on the magazine covers than they do around us; they were also much more prevalent as *Playboy* centrefolds, particularly in the 1970s. It seems that *Playboy*-reading gentlemen certainly prefer blondes …

Sorokowski (2006) tested the influence of hair colour on the perception of a woman's age and physical attractiveness. The results showed without doubt that blond hair has a rejuvenation factor that makes a woman over the age of 25 more attractive – to men of any age. This fact has an evolutionary logic to it. Men want to mate with young women, and one accurate indicator of health and youthfulness is hair. Since hair grows relatively slowly, long lustrous hair is an indicator of several years of healthy living. Hence many women strive to display a shiny mane of shoulder-length hair. But why blond hair in particular? Because blond hair is unique in that it changes relatively quickly, usually turning brown by middle age; thus men who prefer to mate with blonde women are unconsciously indicating their preference for younger women, who are likely to be both healthy and fertile.

We touched on the concept of 'natural' or 'evolutionary' selection in 'The faithful hound' (p54), where this idea is explained – and it is equally relevant in the context of hair colour. It is no coincidence that natural selection in northern Europe and Scandinavia favoured blondes. The climate in this part of the world led women to conceal their bodies under numerous layers of animal skins. Blond hair evolved as one of the few visible signs of good health and youth, and so blonde cavegirls were able to promote themselves more successfully than others. The men who chose blonde young mates were more successful in reproducing than those who chose older partners. Therefore the inherited preference for blond hair, the cultural association of blond hair with youth, and the prevalence of blond hair itself, have all been perpetuated through the centuries – and still exist today. Of course, cavegirls were not able to dye their hair blonde, whereas nowadays women can have any hair colour they choose. Perhaps men's psychology has not evolved quite as quickly as the cosmetics industry: at a subconscious level, some of us may still be fooled by relatively recent inventions, such as hair dye, that didn't exist in our ancestral environment (adapted from Miller and Kanazawa, 2007.)

Another researcher to take an evolutionary view regarding the attractions of blonde women is the Canadian anthropologist Peter Frost (Frost, 2006). Around 11,000 years ago, at the end of the Ice Age, the only food in northern Europe was obtained from hunting among the roaming herds of mammoths, reindeer and bison. This was an extremely hazardous pursuit in which many men perished. As a result, a high female–male ratio became common amongst the tribes, and there was fierce competition among females for the few males who remained. Frost suggests that blond hair and blue eyes evolved in this period, to distinguish certain women from their rivals; lighter hair colours, which started as rare mutations, became popular for breeding and numbers increased dramatically. Frost also cites other sources supporting the hypothesis that blond hair signals high levels of oestrogen, which in turn are indicators of fertility.

There are potential problems with this theory, however. One healthy man can reproduce with lots of females and it is unlikely that strict monogamy was practised in ancient cultures. Therefore a shortage of males would not necessarily lead to increased competition amongst females. A female who can encourage a male to be faithful, treating her preferentially, has a better chance of passing on her genes because her offspring are more likely to survive. However, it is rare in the animal kingdom for females to evolve 'come look at me' adornments in order to catch the best male. It is usually males who develop the tail feathers, the antlers and the urge to fight one another in order to attract females. Nevertheless, it's a neat hypothesis and may explain the speed at which blond hair and blue eyes have evolved. Scientists believe that if the changes had occurred as part of the usual processes of evolution they would have taken 850,000 years to establish.

Another study indicates that men seem to prefer the rarest hair colour, whether it be brown or blond. Thomas Thelen (1983) prepared three series of slides featuring attractive women: one series showed six brunettes, another showed one brunette and five blondes, and a third showed one brunette and eleven blondes. Male subjects then had to choose the woman in each series that they would most like to marry. The result? Preference for the same brunette increased significantly in proportion to the rarity of her hair colour. It's hypothesized that had blondes been in the minority in these slides, a clear preference would have been shown for them: the rarer the hair colour, the more people prefer it. (Try telling that to a redhead.)

Juni and Roth (1985) conducted research into whether blondes would be more likely to be offered help in the street. Two males and two females stopped 72 men and 72 women in the street to ask for their help. For half the interactions, the researchers donned brown wigs; for the other half they wore blond wigs. The study showed that women helped women and men equally, whereas men were more likely to help a woman than another man. At no time in the study was hair colour a significant factor. Perhaps we can deduce from this that the age of chivalry is not dead.

When Lawson (1971) investigated stereotypes associated with hair colour, he found that only blond gentlemen prefer blondes. Rating scales on seven different categories of hair colour were given to 79 male and 161 female undergraduates. The results showed that:

- dark men preferred brunettes;
- blond men were equally divided in their preference for blondes or brunettes;
- blonde, brunette and red-headed women preferred dark men;
- artificial blondes preferred dark and blond men.

One possible reason why men might prefer blondes relates to the fact that blond hair is a recessive trait. If a blonde wife were to be unfaithful, her recessive traits would act as a blank slate: the dominant traits of any adulterous dark-haired partner would be revealed in their offspring, for all to see. Therefore a blonde woman married to a man of similar recessive traits might subconsciously avoid men with dominant traits to have an affair with. Blond men could use this knowledge, perhaps, as a check on the fidelity of their partners.

A study carried out by Peter Ayton of City University claims to have discovered that 'gentlemen no longer prefer blondes' (Unilever, 2005). Ayton suggests that a man's ideal partner is now a brunette – brown hair being perceived as indicative of intelligence and strength in a woman. Researchers showed 1,500 men three pictures of the same female model; the photographs had been digitally enhanced to show the model first as a blonde, then as a brunette and finally as a redhead. The men were then asked to give their impressions of the model's personality based on her hair colour. More than half the men rated the brunette as the most attractive woman, though there were some regional differences: Geordies preferred the redhead (22 per cent) and Yorkshiremen chose the blonde (40 per cent) – proving, perhaps, that there are more gentlemen in Yorkshire. Ayton suggested that although blond hair has traditionally been symbolic of youth and attractiveness, men's preferences are changing: the air of intelligence and sophistication that they now seek is more closely associated with brunettes.

Perhaps the jury is still out. The editors of *Playboy* may be convinced that gentlemen prefer blondes. But brunettes often come out tops in the hair colour desirability lists …

➡ *See also* The dumb blonde; The faithful hound; The gold-digging woman and the looks-obsessed man; The passionate redhead.

The gold-digging woman and the looks-obsessed man

Curvy blonde seeks young-at-heart multimillionaire with GSOH for long-term relationship. Box 1234.

Rich businessman seeks great-looking supermodel for fun in the afternoons. Box 2134.

Ever-increasing divorce rates would suggest that many of us have difficulty in finding our ideal partner. What is the elusive thing we are looking for, and are men and women looking for different things? One way in which psychologists have investigated what people are searching for in a partner is by trawling the content of hundreds of lonely hearts ads. When every word costs money, you must cut to the chase and appeal to your suitors' basic instincts. Therefore the curvy lady whose ad appears above sums up succinctly both what she *wants* (a rich sugar daddy) and what she *offers* (an ample figure and blond hair).

The research of Waynforth and Dunbar (1995) suggests that the male and female stereotypes are generally supported by the evidence that lonely hearts columns provide. Men offer their status at work and their financial prospects and they generally seek attractiveness in women above all else. Women offer their looks, and in a potential partner they seek material resources. Dunbar (1995) confirmed these findings in a follow-up study involving 200 university students, also noting that women look for a sense of commitment. Whilst these findings may not be comforting to unattractive women, they will give hope to ugly but committed men who have good jobs.

Dunbar argues that our sexual preferences have been honed over millions of years of evolution. Women are not too concerned about a man's age, since older men are still capable of fathering children. Men are attracted to good-looking women because attractiveness is a sign of 'good genes' – and since female fertility is closely linked to age, they also tend to show a preference for younger women. But what happens when they are pushed to choose between attractiveness and youth in selecting a long-term partner? A study conducted by George Fieldman, of the Buckinghamshire Chilterns University College, indicates that most men opt for attractiveness (BBC News, 2001). This suggests that the prospect of having attractive children is more appealing to men than that of having many children – since the women of their choice have fewer child-bearing years ahead of them.

Strassberg and Holty (2003) conducted a study of lonely hearts ads posted on the internet. Whilst Waynforth and Dunbar had analysed the content of genuine ads, Strassberg and Holty took another approach: they placed four 'female seeking male' ads, each containing different keywords, on two large internet dating bulletin boards. Together, the four ads generated 500 e-mail responses. Contrary to expectations, the most popular was the one in which the woman described herself as 'financially independent … successful [and] ambitious'. It generated over 50 per cent more responses than the next most popular ad, in which the woman described herself as 'lovely ... attractive and slim'. These findings run counter to the stereotype – at least amongst people using internet dating. Perhaps the men doubted that a woman who really was 'lovely, attractive and slim' would ever need to use this means of finding a partner ...

Is there a strong cultural element to the features we search for in a mate? It seems not. Research evidence the world over usually fits the stereotype. In a comprehensive study of 37 cultures across six continents and five islands, Buss (1989) found that most women in all the cultures involved evaluated prospective male suitors on a cluster of characteristics related to resource potential: good financial prospects, ambition, industriousness, age and emotional maturity. Men, on the other hand, valued potential female partners in terms of 'fecundity' – that is, their ability to produce and care for children. These findings are entirely in accord with the evolutionary perspective. Cunningham (1986) takes this further, observing that men are often attracted to women with infantile features, including large eyes and a small nose, because they associate this 'baby face' look with fertility and good health. Facial symmetry is also a good indicator of attractiveness – probably because it is associated with strong and healthy genes.

Let's look a bit more closely now at different aspects of attractiveness and their evolutionary origins. Clear unwrinkled skin, bright eyes, full lips and glossy hair are obvious indicators of good general health. However, facial appearance is not the only characteristic that provides revealing information to potential mates. Humans find beauty in many other physical attributes – including, for example, the relationship between a woman's hip and waist measurements. Singh (1993) used archival data from the last 50 years to examine the waist–hip ratio (WHR) of beauty contest winners and *Playboy* centrefolds. The perceived attractiveness of most elements of a woman's physique vary over the years, according to fashion. However, Singh found that a woman with a small waist set against full hips was consistently viewed as attractive. He concluded that a WHR of 0.7 is associated with better health and greater reproductive capacity: hence men's preference.

These female proportions and many other physical characteristics that we find attractive are the result of evolutionary selection. Particular facial characteristics and bodily proportions are seen as beautiful because those ancestors who appreciated them produced plenty of healthy offspring, and we have inherited our ancestors' likes and dislikes. Although aspects of a woman's character and behaviour – for example, faithfulness and intelligence – can indicate that she would make a good mother, it is her physical characteristics that are of prime importance to a potential mate. For this reason, it is believed that men see large breasts as an indication of fertility, a thin waist as evidence that a woman is not already pregnant, large buttocks as a sign of fat reserves (which in turn suggest good nutrition) and broad hips as a predictor of effective child-bearing. So it is that men can assess a woman's attractiveness almost immediately.

Women generally make a far greater parental investment than men in the nurturing of their offspring (Buss and Malamuth, 1996). For example, they are more concerned about the provision of material necessities (such as food) and take a greater interest in maintaining the home or territory. They also spend more time teaching their offspring and are more aware of the need to protect them. It is therefore not surprising that women need plenty of time in which to evaluate the resources that a potential mate can offer and are not as strongly influenced by his initial appearance. Men are all too aware of women's focus on their material resources. The 'good genes' hypothesis (Zahavi, 1975) explains why males like to make a splash with their cash and why this might help them to attract a mate. A Ferrari driver, for example, makes a powerful statement about the extent of his own success. This extravagant display, not unlike that of a peacock parading his absurdly long tail, signals to the female that this is a 'high-quality' male with 'good genes' and ample resources. Females value most highly those males who can thrive with the greatest handicap: therefore the Ferrari driver demonstrates that he can spend a fortune on a costly toy while still finding money to live. Only a man in a firm financial position could afford such extravagance.

Again this trend holds true across a variety of cultures. Betzig (1986) reported that in polygamous societies, men with status and wealth have more wives than other men. In a later study, he found that inadequate financial support by husbands was cited as a cause of divorce in many societies around the world – but in no society did men cite inadequate financial support by their wives as grounds for divorce (Betzig, 1989).

A clever test of the hypothesis that men and woman are looking for different characteristics was devised by Townsend and Levy (1990). They presented men and women with photographs of people of the opposite sex who varied both in physical attractiveness and in social status, as indicated by their clothing. In one set of photographs, the models wore low-status clothing (for example, fast-food restaurant uniforms); in another they wore stereotypical 'middle-status' clothing; in the final set they wore designer clothes and accessories. Participants were asked how willing they would be to enter into various types of relationships with the people in the photos. The women found the least physically attractive man the most acceptable to have coffee with, date, have sex with and marry – provided that he wore a Rolex® watch and designer clothes. Men's responses were influenced primarily by physical attractiveness. They were unwilling to date the less attractive woman even if she was wearing designer clothes – which suggests that they had little interest in her social status.

Most of the evidence I have given you about the differing preferences of men and women concentrates on evolutionary factors that revolve around the perpetuation of the species. But relationships are not based entirely on reproductive strategies – they are far more complicated than that. Not everyone is looking for a life partner and many people may have a more short-term approach in which one-night stands predominate. Others may deliberately choose not to have children despite the fact that they are committed to a lifelong partnership.

Setting aside the many variants that different situations and personalities can present us with, we can nevertheless make some general conclusions. We men are shallow in our choice of partner: whilst not necessarily obsessed with a woman's looks, her appearance is extremely important to us. Women are equally shallow: their choice depends primarily on money – and it's true that some may be gold-diggers. So, male reader, consider investing in designer clothes and an expensive car. Ladies, try to improve your looks – but the money you spend on designer clothes is wasted. Now where's that copy of *Autotrader*?

➡ *See also* The gentleman who prefers blondes; The slim and seductive woman; The sower of wild oats.

The good Samaritan

You may know the parable of the good Samaritan, which encourages us, by example, to show compassion to others (Bible, Luke 10.25–37). A man on his way from Jerusalem to Jericho is mugged, robbed and left half-dead. Two religious men pretend not to notice the man and hurry by on the other side of the road. However, a Samaritan, who would have been looked down upon at that time because of his race, carries out some basic first aid, takes the man to an inn, and pays the innkeeper to look after him before continuing his journey.

Conventional wisdom suggests that there are connections between religious belief and kindness or altruism – and by altruism I mean 'an unselfish concern for the welfare of others' (Chambers, 2005). The stereotype is that believers are more generous both with their time and their money. Some studies have shown that they are more likely to work among the poor and needy (Colasanto, 1989), to campaign for social justice and to give away a higher percentage of their income (Myers, 2005).

There are various reasons why religious people may show more altruism than non-religious people. These are some of them:

- Most of the world's major religions actively promote altruism.
- Religious people may believe that they will be rewarded in the afterlife for their altruistic acts.
- There could be a self-select bias – in that altruistic people are more attracted to religions that promote altruism.
- Religion may sometimes prime people to be receptive to altruistic messages, and this may affect their subsequent behaviour.

One famous study that tested the 'good Samaritan principle' was conducted by Darley and Batson (1973), who described the implications of the parable as follows:

> people who encounter a situation possibly calling for a helping response while thinking religious and ethical thoughts will be no more likely to offer aid than persons thinking about something else ... [and] persons encountering a possible helping situation when they are in a hurry will be less likely to offer aid than persons not in a hurry.
>
> Darley and Batson, 1973

To test these hypotheses, Darley and Batson recruited 40 students from the Princeton Theological College. Half the students were given the text of the good Samaritan parable and told that they would be required to deliver a sermon on it; the other half were told that they were to give a talk about their future employment prospects. All the participants were told to report to another building to deliver their talks; however, some were told that they should hurry, while others were led to believe that they had plenty of time to get there. On the way, each student passed a scruffily dressed man slumped in a doorway, head down, eyes closed and not moving. The man was described by the researchers as an 'ambiguous figure', possibly needing help, possibly drunk, possibly dangerous – much like the man on the road to Jericho. As each student passed, the man coughed twice and moaned.

Only 40 per cent of the theology students offered to help the victim. The only factor that seemed to predict helping behaviour was how much time they believed they had to get to the other building. Students thinking about the good Samaritan parable were no more likely to help than those about to give a talk on their job prospects. Being primed with religious thoughts did not lead the students to act more altruistically.

It is not always easy for people to understand that others may behave altruistically because of their religious views. Dixon and Abbey (2000) conducted a study among doctors who regularly carried out psychiatric assessments of potential organ donors. Most potential donors come forward because they are related to the person needing the transplant. In the study, however, researchers presented the doctors with case studies in which each of the possible donors described his or her generous offer as having its origins in religious belief. Many of the doctors reacted negatively to these case studies, which suggests that they found religious beliefs a strange reason for acting altruistically.

A study conducted by Koenig *et al.* (2007) set out to test whether religiousness has a positive influence on 'prosocial' behaviours – again, these are altruistic actions taken for no reason other than to help someone. Koenig also wanted to discover the extent to which these associations are due to genetic make-up or environment. Religiousness, antisocial behaviour and altruistic behaviour were assessed by self-report in a sample of 165 identical and 100 non-identical adult male twins. Religiousness, both retrospective and current, was shown to be negatively correlated with antisocial behaviour and positively correlated with altruistic behaviour – though both sets of correlations were modest. This suggests that the more people reported themselves to be religious, the more they also described themselves as altruistic and the less they portrayed themselves as antisocial. The use of twins in this study allowed many of the effects of environment and heredity to be disentangled. As a result, Koenig was able to make a case for the existence of genes that predispose people towards religiousness. Perhaps the same factors that influence religiousness also increase altruism, and the connection between the two is further strengthened by the fact that, since most religions promote altruism, altruistic people are attracted to religion.

A report by Brooks (2003) showed some marked differences in the amount that religious Americans give, of both their money and their time, when compared with others. In Brooks' study, those people who attended a religious service at least once a week were classed as 'religious'. This group were 25 per cent more likely than non-religious people to donate money (91 per cent compared to 66 per cent); they were also 23 per cent more likely to volunteer time to help a charity (67 per cent compared to 44 per cent).

A look at another group of religious people paints a rather less flattering picture. Doctors work in a profession that is intrinsically altruistic (in that its aim is to provide care for the sick) yet can also encourage selfishness (since it pays a high wage and denotes high status). It might therefore be expected that doctors who hold religious views might want to offset their high salary and status by working more with underprivileged groups. A study by Curlin *et al.* (2007) suggests this is not the case. Of the 1,144 US physicians who were surveyed, 26 per cent taken from the general population reported working in 'underserved' communities – that is, among people who have poor access to healthcare, usually because of poverty. This percentage was roughly the same among doctors with religious beliefs: 27 per cent of doctors with low religiosity and 29 per cent of the highly religious worked with the underprivileged.

The parable of the good Samaritan suggests that a person who appears religious may not necessarily act in an altruistic way. In fact, research indicates that people who hold religious beliefs are a little more altruistic than non-believers, although this is certainly not true in all cases. People who hold religious beliefs might actually be considered *less* altruistic if they believe that they'll be rewarded in the afterlife for their kind deeds: stacking up credits in this life to use in the next may not count as entirely unselfish behaviour.

In conclusion, there may be a weak correlation between religious belief and kindness, but one doesn't necessarily trigger the other. Of course, we have not considered the reverse side of the religion–altruism coin, where we may see evil acts or atrocities (such as the Crusades, or the 9/11 World Trade Center attacks) perpetrated by individuals who claim to have strong religious beliefs. But the occasions when religion actively promotes evil acts are mercifully rare.

The gourmet Frenchman, the tight-fisted Scot and the serious German

Heaven is a place where the police are English, the cooks are French, the mechanics are German, the lovers are Italian and everything is organized by the Swiss. Hell is a place where the police are German, the cooks are English, the mechanics are French, the lovers are Swiss, and everything is organized by the Italians.

As it is politically incorrect to even think of discussing national stereotypes, I embark on this subject with much trepidation. The old joke above seems the safest place to start, with its gentle humour based on sweeping generalizations about the qualities of various nationalities. There are, of course, many other stereotypes associated with nationalities. The Spanish leave everything until *mañana* (tomorrow); the English are polite and love queuing; the Irish have the gift of the gab and enjoy a drink or two; Americans are fat and loud. There are, of course, at least as many variations between people within any one national group as there are between different nationalities; however, labelling a particular view as a stereotype doesn't necessarily mean that the observations on which it is based are entirely untrue.

How did national stereotypes evolve in the first place? There is a different story behind each one, but it is thought that some are based on certain values that are held in particularly high esteem within a nation; they have their roots in historical truth and have persisted despite changing circumstances. For example,

Americans are often stereotyped as freethinkers who place great emphasis on freedom of expression and individualism. These values may originate from the experiences of the pioneers in the Wild West who extolled such virtues: the First Amendment to the US Constitution emphasizes the many freedoms that its citizens enjoy, including freedom of religion, freedom of speech and freedom of the press. Another possibility is that one small aspect of a national stereotype may be true and this is then generalized incorrectly. For example, Italians use a lot of hand gestures in their conversations, which may have prompted the stereotype that they are passionate and hot-tempered. In this case, a behavioural observation has been wrongly generalized into a personality trait.

It may be that the stereotypes persist because we believe that we see the evidence for them on a daily basis during our interactions with people from different nations. Every Scotsman who doesn't rush to the bar is seen as tight-fisted, every German who doesn't laugh at a joke has no sense of humour, and so on. A phenomenon known as the 'confirmation bias' may encourage us to believe these stereotypes to be accurate. Confirmation bias is a type of selective thinking whereby we tend to notice and look for evidence that confirms our beliefs, and ignore or undervalue the relevance of anything that contradicts them.

One of the first pieces of research to investigate 'confirmation bias' was initiated by Peter Wason (1960), who presented participants with a triplet of numbers (for example, 2, 4, 6) and asked them to work out the rule that had produced it. They were allowed to identify the rule by proposing more triplets that would follow it. (The correct answer is at the foot of this page.[1]) Most people tackled the problem by hypothesizing a rule (say, successive even numbers) and producing only those triplets that are consistent with it (for example, 6, 8, 10). After a number of affirmative trials, participants then put forward their rule as the solution. In most cases, because participants did not generate any triplets that were inconsistent with their proposed rule, they prevented themselves from realizing that they were incorrect. In other words, they looked for confirmatory evidence only. Thus if they generated triplets to fit their hypothesized rule (say, successive even numbers), they did not test other similar rules (such as an increase in twos, any three positive numbers, and so on). The key is to test the hypothesis by deliberately selecting triplets that reveal the rule to be wrong (Nickerson, 1998). From this demonstration, it is clear that looking only for confirmatory evidence is misguided: it is more important to examine and take note of evidence to the contrary. Perhaps similar confirmatory bias occurs with national stereotypes.

Kunda (1990) suggests (somewhat ironically) that the reason we ignore or discount evidence that runs against our expectations is that we believe it is important to hold beliefs that are justified. We value consistency in our beliefs to such an extent that we choose to ignore inconsistencies. This is a real worry if our beliefs are little more than prejudices. However, Gilovich (1993) believes that there is a less sinister explanation for the confirmation bias, arguing that 'the most likely reason for the excessive influence of confirmatory information is that it is easier to deal with cognitively'. Stereotypes certainly make for a simpler view of the world.

A study conducted by Terracciano and McCrae (2005)

---

[1] The simple rule is: any three ascending numbers.

investigated stereotypes in 49 cultures throughout the world. In this study, researchers asked nearly 4,000 participants to describe the 'typical' member of their own culture. They then compared these average, typical or stereotyped national descriptions with the results of personality measures previously administered in these countries. There was little agreement between the two descriptions. For example, Americans rated the typical American as assertive, whereas Canadians rated the typical Canadian as submissive, but in fact Americans and Canadians achieve virtually identical scores on psychometric measures of assertiveness. Indians rate the typical Indian as unconventional and open to a wide range of new experiences, but personality measures suggest that Indians are conventional compared to many other nationalities. If people have inaccurate views of their own national characteristics, it is hardly surprising that outsiders have an equally poor understanding of them. The researchers concluded that national stereotypes are not generalizations based on real observations of people in those countries, but unfounded stereotypes. They suggest that national stereotypes are social constructions, probably based on the socioeconomic conditions, history, customs, myths and values of a culture.

Let's now examine some of the facts that relate to national stereotypes – starting with those concerning alcohol consumption. Surely the Irish, with their home-produced Guinness® and their love of the *craic* (noisy carousing and banter, usually in a pub) must be the most bibulous European nation? Not so. According to World Drink Trends (Commission for Distilled Spirits, 2004), the Irish come third in the drinking stakes after the inhabitants of Hungary and Luxembourg, who each consumed the equivalent of twelve litres of pure alcohol per person during 2002. Another

The gourmet Frenchman ...

....

stereotype suggests that Germany is the economic powerhouse of Europe. Actually this is not the case: Ireland and Spain have had faster-growing gross domestic product (GDP) figures in recent years and yet their national stereotypes would not support this evidence. Where is the business and financial centre of Europe? Switzerland, surely, where everything runs like clockwork? Actually no, it's London. What about all those Americans: aren't most of them fat? Yes, there is an element of truth here: 119 million adults (64.5 per cent) in the USA are either overweight or obese (BBC News, 2005) and the figures (in both senses of the word) are growing fast.

Returning to the old joke that I quoted earlier, would it really be hell if the Germans ran the police force? I think not. In the meantime, Gordon Ramsay could supervise the English cooks. After all, Ramsay (a Scot from the land of the deep-fried Mars® bar) has been showered with Michelin® stars and is recognized as one of the top chefs in the world. And are the Italians really so poor at organization? They run highly successful engineering and chemical industries and they weren't too bad in the past at organizing conquests of other countries. Remember the 'What did the Romans ever do for us?' scene in *Monty Python's Life of Brian*, directed by Terry Jones (1979)? In answer to this question, the assembled crowd reluctantly agree that the Romans developed aqueducts, sanitation, roads, irrigation, medicine, education and, most important of all, wine.

The trouble with most stereotypes is that they are negative and may simply reinforce racist views. Being thought of as efficient and hardworking (Germans) or good at sport and enjoying a carefree outdoor life (Australians) are exceptional stereotypes because they have a positive bias. (Inevitably, perhaps, the Germans and

Australians are branded with negative stereotypes too.) Since national stereotypes are rarely positive, perhaps it's time to stop perpetuating them and accept that every nationality is a diverse mix of individuals. The British are sometimes stereotyped as xenophobes, with an abiding suspicion of all things foreign. Is that so? I've never heard such an inaccurate stereotype – it must have been a foreigner who invented it. After all, being British is all about driving in a German car to an Irish pub for a Belgian beer, grabbing an Indian curry on the way home, and sitting on Swedish furniture to watch US shows or French footballers on a Japanese TV.

➡ *See also* The football hooligan.

The grim North

he origin of the phrase 'It's grim up North' probably dates back to the 18th and 19th centuries, when the northern cities of England were the powerhouses of the industrial revolution and giant manufacturing industries spewed out vast quantities of dirt and pollution. Nowadays, with Britain becoming ever more reliant on the service industry, most of the 'dark satanic mills' have disappeared. So is the 'grim North' stereotype still relevant today? Having been born in Bournemouth, one of the most southerly towns in Britain, and spent most of my adult life in or near Southampton, I may not be the best qualified to comment. Therefore, in the interests of fairness, I will focus on giving you all the facts that I can concerning the North–South divide.

According to UK Government figures (Office of the Deputy Prime Minister, 2003), there remain clear differences between the North and the South as regards quality of life. The South has a higher economic output (gross domestic product per head is £10,024 in the North East compared to £15,098 in the South East), higher employment rates, higher levels of educational attainment, less poverty, fewer robberies (apart from the hotspot of London) and less car crime (although London rates match those of Yorkshire and the Humber). People living in the South seem generally to experience better health and a life expectancy that extends two years beyond that of people living in the North. Levels of heart disease in particular are higher in the North, with Middlesbrough in Teeside topping the list. House prices in the South are way above those in the North – with the exception of a few property treasure troves such as Alderley Edge in Cheshire, which is said to have more millionaires living in it than any other English village, town or city apart from London's Mayfair.

Of course, the fact that the statistics appear to support the 'grim North' stereotype is of little or no daily concern to people who live there. Where exactly does 'the North' begin anyway? Danny Dorling of the University of Sheffield argues that the North–South dividing line has moved in recent years, due to a number of socioeconomic developments – including rising house prices, increased life expectancy and voting patterns. Dorling believes that, contrary to popular opinion, the divide no longer begins at the Watford Gap but at the Severn estuary; it then heads up towards the Humber in a zigzag diagonal line, hitting the coast just south of Grimsby. The Midlands, Dorling believes, is now a mix of North and South: 'the South has a few pockets of poverty in a sea of affluence, whereas the North has a few pockets of affluence in a sea of poverty'. He suggests that only one other line in Europe has ever had such a strong influence on one's life chances: the 'iron curtain' that once separated East and West Germany (Day, 2007).

This brings me to the interesting point that North–South issues are not restricted to England. In both the United States and Italy there are marked North–South divides – although in these countries the more prosperous North seems to feel that it has the upper hand over its poor relatives in the South. In Italy, the North–South divide is marked by partisan politics. Politicians in the Lega Nord (Northern League) campaign for separation from their cousins in the South, who are often referred to as *terroni* ('people of the earth'). Thankfully there is no support for North–South separation in England – yet.

You might think that the 'grim North' stereotype could be true on a Europe-wide perspective, with the people living in sunny Mediterranean countries being happier than those in the colder climes of northern Europe. This is not borne out by the research. A European Social Survey carried out by Cambridge University asked people from different countries to rate their happiness on a scale of one to ten, with ten being the happiest (Charter, 2007). Italy, Greece and Portugal were amongst the lowest-scoring countries with Sweden, Finland and the Netherlands being at the top – just below the table-topper, Denmark. What is it, for them, that leads to happiness? Not sunshine, but trust in government, the police and each other. The UK was in a not-so-great ninth place out of 15 European Union countries.

What about that widespread belief that suicides are more common amongst those who live in northern climes? It is certainly true that there is a negative correlation between the numbers of hours of daylight and suicide rates: as daylight hours decrease, suicide rates increase. This applies particularly to places in the far north, such as parts of Scandinavia and Alaska – and it may be that people who suffer from seasonal affective disorder (SAD) experience greater depression as a result of the lack of sunlight. However, there are marked differences in suicide rates between different countries, and this suggests differences in reporting methods – and possibly in attitudes to suicide. In many Scandinavian countries, for example, the stigma associated with a death being recorded as a suicide is relatively low in comparison with some other countries (Soreff, 2006), and this may account for the higher figures. However, within the UK, where reporting methods (and presumably attitudes) are the same throughout, the highest suicide rates are still recorded in more northerly regions. Scotland's suicide rates are twice those in England: the highest rate of male suicide in the UK is recorded in Shetland (47.5 per 100,000) and the highest rate of female suicide is found in Glasgow (15.8 per 100,000).

When I started writing I believed that I wouldn't find much

support for the 'grim North' stereotype. I was wrong: many of the quality of life measures suggest that the North–South divide still exists – in favour of the South. But the North nevertheless has much in its favour. In a BBC TV programme with accompanying book, entitled *It's (Not) Grim Up North* (Holder, 2005), various well-known personalities from the North extolled the virtues of everything north of the Watford Gap. One of the main points made was that although the South may experience better weather, the North is renowned for the friendliness of the people. What's more, many Northern cities are praised for their urban regeneration projects: cities such as Manchester, Liverpool, Newcastle and Leeds ('Britain's Barcelona') are described as 'unmissable' places to visit (Lonely Planet, 2005). All this suggests that it is certainly less grim up North than once it was – in fact, the alternative phrase 'It's great up North' may be more accurate. But only time will tell if Bradford is to be the new Tuscany.

The headache-prone woman

One of the oldest stereotypes there is involves a husband snuggling up to his wife in bed – only to be told, 'Not tonight, I've got a headache'. Don't be too upset about this, gentlemen, it is more than likely that your wife is telling the truth. Research suggests that a woman is three times more likely than a man to  have a headache or migraine, although the difference starts to decrease after the age of 40 (Stewart *et al.*, 1994). Women also report more severe levels of pain, worse symptoms (including nausea and vomiting) and headaches that tend to last longer.

So why are headaches more common among women than men? The day-to-day stresses of work and family life certainly contribute to headaches; however, since these stresses are experienced by both sexes, they do not really account for the fact that women experience headaches more frequently. A more likely cause of regular migraine-type headaches in women is the hormones whose levels fluctuate at certain times of the month and at different stages of life. The strength of this hypothesis is borne out by the fact that over half of the women who suffer from migraine headaches usually experience them around the time of their period. Some women develop migraines only when they start taking birth control pills; others develop them when they enter the menopause. All this evidence suggests a link between headaches and hormonal change. It seems logical, therefore, that research investigating the most effective drugs for migraine in women should focus on hormonal treatment. One hormonal treatment that does seem to be effective is pregnancy. Several studies have shown that 70 per cent of women who suffer from migraines note an improvement during pregnancy; however, ten per cent of women experience their first migraine at this time (Lance, 1982).

Occasionally a couple's lovemaking may come to an abrupt end when one partner says, 'No more tonight, I've now got a headache' – and this is more likely to be the man. Sex headaches (coital cephalgia) are mercifully rare and account for only one out of every 360 headaches. These headaches, which vary considerably in severity, initially cause pain at the base of the skull, but can spread all over the head. They usually interrupt the proceedings when two people are in the midst of having sex – but have also been known to occur earlier, when they are merely getting into position. Sex headaches are a subset of a larger family known as 'exertional headaches', which are caused by exercise. The reason why these headaches are more common among men than women is unclear; however, it may be linked to the fact that a man is more likely to be the active partner during sex. There are other sex headaches known as 'orgasmic headaches', which – as you might suspect – are sudden and severe; these too are more common in men than in women, perhaps because men are more likely to experience an orgasm. Some orgasmic headaches have been known to last a day or two. Explaining the reasons for one's absence from work must be tricky in these circumstances.

But it's not all bad news when it comes to headaches and sex. There is some evidence that sex can alleviate the pain of headaches and migraines. The neurotransmitter serotonin, which transmits nerve impulses in the brain and is thought to have a biochemical effect on mood, is less active during a migraine attack. Having an orgasm releases serotonin and activates those pathways in the brain that may help to loosen the grip of the migraine. Of course, to borrow from another stereotype, there's no guarantee that a woman will have an orgasm during sex – and faked orgasms only work for faked headaches.

➡ *See also* The emotional woman; The sex-obsessed man.

The intelligent classical music lover

I've been listening to the Brit rock band Coldplay and am finding it difficult to write. So I'm going to play some Mozart instead. Why? For two reasons. First, many people believe that classical music is of a higher calibre than other types of music, and is appreciated by more intelligent people. There is a kind of anti-pop prejudice at work here: if you listen to classical music, you're clever; if you listen to pop music, you're dim. Secondly, some people take further this train of thought, claiming that listening to Mozart in particular helps to develop intelligence: his Sonata in D for Two Pianos (K448) and his Piano Concerto No. 23 in A major (K488) are the pieces typically referred to as beneficial.

Listening to classical music is often seen as 'intellectual', relaxing and generally good for our intelligence. Much of the research into its effects is based on a particular theory concerning the workings of the cerebral cortex – the part of the brain that helps with, among other things, motor control, speech, memory and auditory reception. This theory, the 'trion model', was developed by neurobiologist Gordon Shaw at the University of California-Irvine. Shaw showed that the brain cell activity that takes place when subjects are listening to music is similar to that which occurs when they perform spatial tasks (Leng and Shaw, 1991).

The term 'Mozart effect' dates back to a study published in the journal *Nature*. The study claimed that listening to a Mozart sonata for ten minutes enabled adults to improve their scores on a spatial intelligence test (Rauscher *et al.*, 1993). Rauscher and Shaw hypothesized that listening to certain types of complex music may 'warm-up' neural transmitters inside the cerebral cortex and thereby improve spatial performance. Rauscher later suggested that rats exposed *in utero* or as newborns to the music of Mozart were quicker at learning to navigate a maze than others not similarly exposed (Rauscher, 2006). Campbell (1997) sums up well the claims of the 'Mozart effect', suggesting that it

> represents the general use of music to reduce stress, depression, or anxiety, induce relaxation or sleep, activate the body, and improve memory or awareness. Innovative and experimental uses of music and sound can improve listening disorders, dyslexia, attention deficit disorder, autism, and other mental and physical disorders and injuries.

> Campbell, 1997

These researchers were not alone in their enthusiasm for the 'Mozart effect'. Parents and parents-to-be soon began to play Mozart to their babies, both before and after birth, as a 'quick fix' for producing intelligent children – or so they hoped. Many pregnant women welcomed with open arms the idea of putting their feet up and treating their baby to some *in utero* Mozart. Belief in the 'Mozart effect' spread rapidly, offering a novel answer – which had apparently sprung from academic science – to a genuine question: how can I help develop my child's intelligence? A new and lucrative industry came into being with the sole purpose of extolling its virtues. Campbell wrote two books on the subject and created a number of related 'Mozart effect' products.

Let's investigate whether this common belief stands up to closer scrutiny. One study that supports the 'Mozart effect' was conducted by Wilson and Brown (1997), who tested the spatial reasoning of 22 college students. The students were asked to complete pen-and-paper mazes as quickly as possible in an eight-minute period; half had previously listened to Mozart while the remainder had listened to other music or none. The average student completed 2.68 mazes in eight minutes after listening to Mozart; students who had listened to other music completed 2.2 and a control group who had sat in silence completed 1.73.

Jenkins (2001) suggests that listening to music primes the activation of those areas of the brain that are concerned with spatial reasoning. Scans have shown that we use many different parts of our brain to listen to music: rhythm and pitch tend to be processed on the left side, tone and melody on the right. We use some of these same parts of the brain to visualize and manipulate spatial patterns over time. Jenkins also reports evidence of the 'Mozart effect' among people with epilepsy. In 23 of 29 epileptic patients who listened to the Sonata in D for Two Pianos (K448), there was a significant decrease in epileptiform activity as shown by electroencephalogram (EEG). Some individual patients showed especially striking improvement (Hughes *et al.*, 1998).

Is it specifically the music of Mozart that causes people to perform better in cognitive tasks? Probably not: many of the Mozart pieces used in the research are upbeat and energetic and it may be these qualities, rather than the fact that the music is Mozart's, that explain the improved performance. Personal preference for the music heard in 'Mozart effect' testing may also increase spatial reasoning test scores (Nantais and Schellenberg, 1999).

Having introduced this whisper of doubt as to whether or not the 'Mozart effect' is related to Mozart at all, I must now disillusion you further. Many believe that the results of the original research were simplified for a lay audience and then simplified again by public retelling – and the more times a person tells a story, the more he or she becomes convinced that it is true (Bangerter and Heath, 2004). There is therefore some unease in the research community concerning the original findings of Rauscher and his colleagues. 'Mozart effect' critics have claimed that listening to the music of Mozart (or any other classical composers, for that matter) may simply cause a shift in participants' arousal and mood, which in turn increases their spatial intelligence test scores (Steele, 2006; Thompson *et al.*, 2001). When the effect of this mood shift is incorporated in the data, the 'Mozart effect' disappears.

Other researchers slowly began to check on the power of the 'Mozart effect'. Follow-up studies could not replicate the original and a 1999 review of all previous studies concluded that any effect, if it existed at all, was negligible. There was a difference of only 1.4 general intelligence quotient (IQ) points between participants listening to Mozart and those who had sat in silence (Chabris, 1999). Steele (2006) claimed that since rats are born deaf, they couldn't even have heard the music in that particular experiment (Rauscher, 2006).

Strangely, public belief in the 'Mozart effect' continued to grow despite the raising of many doubts and concerns. The original research became so completely misquoted that many believed the 'Mozart effect' to be most powerful for newborn infants, despite the fact that there is no evidence for this – and the majority of the research has focused on undergraduates. Even now, books on the 'Mozart effect' continue to be published and CDs produced, many of them targeted at pushy parents. In 1998 the US state of Georgia gave classical music CDs to all new mothers: time will tell us how effective this has been ...

More research may one day help determine the effects, if any, that listening to music has on cognitive processing and abilities. As for me, well I've carried on listening to Mozart throughout the writing of this piece. I don't think it has helped much, although it has been pleasant. Now for something else that is upbeat and energetic – the 1970s heavy metal band Black Sabbath.

The lazy fatty

Do you know someone who is a couch potato? Look at the picture and think about the image for a moment. It's not couch celery, couch string bean or even couch banana: the image is of someone rounded, perhaps a bit lumpy – fat and lazy. One

stereotype associated with fatties is that they are obese simply because they are lazy, and a common exhortation to the overweight is 'eat less, move more'. But is it true that fat people are simply lazy, or is this just one aspect of a more general anti-fat bias?

There is a (suitably large) body of evidence suggesting that most of us are biased against overweight and obese people. Perhaps before going further I should make a distinction between the two. The scientific way to measure obesity is to calculate one's body mass index (BMI). This is done by dividing your weight (in kilograms) by your height (in metres) squared. In the UK, people with a BMI of between 25 and 30 are said to be overweight; those with a BMI above 30 are classed as obese; those with a BMI of 40 or more are described as morbidly obese (NHS Direct, 2008).

The evolutionary explanation for obesity is relatively straightforward. In the environment in which we evolved, natural selection shaped appetite regulation mechanisms. In times of famine, it was a case of 'survival of the fattest'. However, it was difficult to build up surplus fat because we often had to walk vast distances to find food. In times of plenty, it was prudent to eat as much as possible – particularly fat and sugar – and to save energy by being lazy, thereby wasting fewer calories. This system worked fine on the plains of Africa, but it doesn't work so well in Neasden, where the local supermarket is open 24/7 and you can order online without moving from your sofa. Now that we have an unlimited diet, the consumption of high-calorie, high-fat food that we do not need has resulted in an epidemic of diseases. Adult obesity is increasing at an alarming rate. In the UK, obesity rates have almost quadrupled over the last 25 years, and 22 per cent of men and 23 per cent of women are now classified as obese. Obesity dramatically increases mortality rates, with an estimated 9,000 deaths each year attributed to obesity alone; in addition, obese people are more likely to suffer from diabetes, heart disease, strokes, cancer, depression and osteoarthritis. Nesse (2001) claims that natural selection will eventually fix this 'design problem', but it may take hundreds or thousands of generations to do so.

Medical effects to one side, how are the obese treated by the rest of society? Obesity is a difficult feature to conceal and body shape often dominates our perception of a person – blocking out other more important characteristics, such as personality or temperament. Regardless of gender, age and ethnicity there is a general tendency to express aversion towards obese persons. Study after study has shown obesity to be wrongly associated with negative stereotypes, particularly in the West. For example, overweight individuals may be stereotyped as morally and emotionally impaired, socially handicapped (Crandall and Biernat, 1990), devoid of sexuality (Millman, 1980), lazy, unattractive, unhappy, unpopular and sloppy (Tiggemann and Rothblum, 1988; Cogan *et al.*, 1996).

Perhaps the most damaging stereotype of all is that obese people have only themselves to blame for their condition and are too weak-willed to regulate their eating behaviour (Crandall, 1994;

Crandall and Biernat, 1990). It is this that distinguishes obesity stereotyping from most other forms of prejudice. Whereas many physical attributes are not within the control of the individual, obesity is often viewed in a different light; this arises from the popular belief that the major causes of obesity are eating too much and exercising too little. Psychological studies into various stigmatizing conditions have looked at how blame is attributed to individuals. They found that when a 'negative' condition such as obesity is attributed to a controllable cause, people make negative judgements and have negative emotional responses to it (Weiner *et al.*, 1988). Some studies with adults have confirmed that negative attitudes to overweight people are significantly correlated with the perceived lack of control over their own weight (Allison *et al.*, 1991; Crandall, 1994).

Following on from this, the term 'fundamental attribution error' (or 'over-attribution effect') has been coined to describe the tendency people have to blame a person's behaviour (for example, eating too much) on particular personality traits (for example, laziness) rather than on the social and/or environmental factors that might also play a part. This error of judgement occurs when we extrapolate from a measurable characteristic (for example, fat) to an unrelated characteristic (for example, lazy). It is easy to understand how the 'eating too much and exercising too little' hypothesis is formed and has spread. However, this attribution of responsibility is not often borne out by objective data from medical studies involving twins, which demonstrate that the tendency to obesity is often caused by genetic factors or metabolic dysfunctions (Stunkard *et al.*, 1986).

So how do our anti-fat attitudes manifest themselves? Research has shown that the negative associations begin early in life. Turnbull *et al.* (2000) asked 25 children aged between two and five years to associate particular personal, behavioural and social traits to some doll figures, which varied in body shape and gender. Far more negative traits were ascribed to the fat dolls, and more negative traits were ascribed to fat females than fat males. Research by Rothblum (1993) suggests that when given pictures of children in wheelchairs, missing limbs, on crutches, facially disfigured or obese, most children indicate that the person they would least like to play with is the fat child (Rothblum, 1993).

Anesbury and Tiggemann (2000) sought to redress anti-fat stereotyping in children. Forty-two children were given lessons that explained the difficulties of weight control in the hope that they might be less inclined to stereotype fat people as a result. After the lessons, the children showed more knowledge of this aspect of obesity than a control group; however, they did not show less anti-fat stereotyping. Well that's another stereotype: children can be cruel... and if children can be cruel, so can parents. One study showed that fat daughters were far less likely to receive financial help from their parents to support them through college. Crandall (1995) surveyed 1,029 college students and 3,386 high school students and found that the weight of the female students was the only factor to affect the level of parental funding. Funding levels remained completely unaffected by other factors such as parental income, ability to pay, ethnicity, family size or number of children attending college. Crandall reported,

> If you believe the fat stereotype and if you believe it is the daughter's fault that she is fat, the less likely you are to believe that she would benefit from higher education.
>
> Crandall, 1995

The fact that no such pattern was found in the funding that parents provided for their obese sons suggests that weight stereotypes are applied more readily to women than to men; this shocking finding illustrates how deeply embedded the anti-fat stereotype may be. College admission tutors are equally susceptible to such attitudes. Research has found that prestigious colleges accept fewer fat high-school students, even when these students do not differ from their average-weight classmates in terms of school performance, academic qualifications or application rates to college (Crandall, 1995). Once these obese students graduate their battle continues in occupational settings. Venturini *et al.* (2006) showed that fat people are usually associated with jobs that require little interpersonal contact. In many recruitment situations they are rejected simply because as overweight people they are not seen as possessing the personal characteristics needed.

It seems that virtually everyone holds anti-fat attitudes. Teachman and Brownell (2001) found that even those healthcare professionals who spend all their time treating obesity display strong negative attitudes towards obese people. In this case, however, the negative associations tend to be implicit rather than explicit: for example, they might not openly confess to seeing fat people as lazy, but when told to match two paired words by pressing buttons, they match them more quickly if 'fat' is paired with 'bad' or 'lazy' rather than 'good' or 'motivated'.

I suspect that you will not be convinced by the argument that obesity may be due primarily to genetic factors. As we have already seen, the research demonstrates that stereotypes about weight develop early in life; they are also difficult to change and are held by both normal weight and overweight individuals (Crandall and Biernat, 1990). Therefore we are not surprised that the NHS Direct helpline suggests, 'The best way of tackling obesity is to reduce the amount of calories that you eat and exercise more' (NHS Direct, 2008). But we are amazed by the medical research suggesting that obesity is often outside an individual's perceived control – and we may be able to give evidence to the contrary.

My friend Neil used to surf (badly), climb and generally keep fit until his career led him into a more sedentary lifestyle. When he went for a medical check-up, he was alarmed to discover that he was obese. He immediately took up climbing again, visited the gym weekly and watched his diet – and he is now back to his old weight. This, together with countless other examples, shows that not all obesity is beyond an individual's control: 'Eat less, move more' works well for many. However, there are social and psychological factors that can influence an individual's motivation and his or her ability to exercise control; add to these a genetic or metabolic disorder, and control of one's own weight may be impossible. It is for the individual to decide whether to investigate the possible cause of the obesity and to ascertain the most suitable way of living with it – or overcoming it. It is not our place to stereotype all fat people as lazy just because weight can sometimes be modified by exercise and diet. Perhaps it is we, the judgemental onlookers, who have the problem.

Although research suggests that even obese people hold anti-fat attitudes (Crandall, 1994), not everyone thinks like this. In the USA, the National Association to Advance Fat Acceptance (NAAFA, 2008) actively works towards providing equal opportunities for fat people and improving their quality of life. There are also individuals who, without campaigning or making weight a political issue, simply view fatness as a positive attribute. For example, the so-called 'chubby chaser' tends to be a man with a preference for overweight women, whom he may refer to as BBWs (big, beautiful women).

There is strong social pressure to suppress discrimination made on the basis of race or gender, but there is no such pressure to quash anti-fat attitudes. Some comedians who wouldn't dream of making a racist joke are perfectly happy to raise a laugh at the expense of fat people. Jimmy Carr told the following joke during the Royal Variety Performance in 2002: 'Someone came up to me last week and complained about a joke, quite a big-boned girl. She said: "I think you're fattist!" I said: "No, I think you're fattest!"'

But being fat is no laughing matter – and neither is anti-fat prejudice. In order to limit the stereotyping of obesity, people need to become more aware of the difficulties that fat people face and perhaps media and education programmes need to address associated beliefs and attitudes. Couch potato? Remember what a hard-working vegetable that potato is – it gets baked, mashed, and turned into dauphinois … oh, and there's chips. But perhaps we should avoid chips …

➡ *See also* The gold-digging woman and the looks-obsessed man; The slim and seductive woman; The slothful student.

The lying politician

I did not have sexual relations with that woman, Miss Lewinsky. I never told anybody to lie, not a single time – never. These allegations are false.

Bill Clinton, Washington DC, 26 January 1998

The above is a good example of a politician telling a direct lie. However, there are many other occasions when politicians may, to use their parlance, choose to be 'economical with the truth' (a phrase made famous by the then British Cabinet Secretary Sir Robert Armstrong during the *Spycatcher* trial in 1986, and further developed by the MP Alan Clark, shown here, as being 'economical with the actualité'). To be fair, there are also times when they act in good faith on inaccurate intelligence or make decisions which later prove to be unwise. Nevertheless, whenever a politician's honesty is called into question, groundlessly or otherwise, there is heated public debate.

Numerous political incidents within living memory have caused us to doubt the integrity of politicians. During the Falklands War in 1982, the Argentinian battleship *General Belgrano* was torpedoed by the British submarine HMS *Conqueror*. The battleship appeared to be sailing away from the war zone at the time; therefore a statement that it was not doing so provoked intense political discussion. More recently, Prime Minister Tony

Blair claimed that Saddam Hussein's military planning would enable some of Iraq's weapons of mass destruction to be ready for use within 45 minutes of an order being issued. When doubt was expressed as to the veracity of this claim, a public uproar followed.

My purpose here is not to speculate on which politicians may have lied and which have not. Instead I want to think about the origins of lying, why all of us do it and why some politicians may be particularly attracted to this form of subterfuge. Before I go any further you might be interested to know that politicians are not the only species capable of lying: other animals do the same – for example, some female birds pretend to have damaged wings in order to lure predators away from their own nests. Evidence also suggests that great apes are able to lie. A captive gorilla called Koko was taught American Sign Language (ASL) by psychologist Francine ('Penny') Patterson. One day, after Koko had thrown a tantrum and broken a sink in the laboratory, the gorilla signed in ASL, 'The cat did it' – thus blaming her pet kitten for the damage (Patterson, 1987).

The German philosopher Friedrich Nietzsche (1844–1900) believed that the lie is a necessary condition of life for all of us. In 1996, Bella DePaulo of the University of Virginia put this to the test. She asked 147 people between the ages of 18 and 71 to keep a diary of all the lies they told during the course of one week. For the purposes of the research, a lie was defined as a statement that deliberately misleads and conveys a false impression; false compliments (for example, 'Nice haircut!') were classed as white lies, and were not counted. The researchers found that the majority of participants lied at least once or twice a day. Both men and women lied in approximately one-fifth of their social exchanges lasting ten or more minutes; over the course of a week they deceived about 30 per cent of those with whom they interacted on a one-to-one level (DePaulo *et al.*, 1996).

There are some professions where a certain amount of lying is expected: estate agents, barristers, used car salesmen and advertising executives all turn a tidy profit peddling what some may see as half truths. But what about the rest of us? Is lying an acceptable behaviour or not? Psychologist Leonard Saxe pointed out that, throughout our lives, we receive conflicting messages about lying (Science Blog, 2004). Although we're told from birth that telling the truth is important, society often discourages us from doing so. Very young children are unable to lie convincingly because they find it difficult to see things from the perspective of another person, which is a prerequisite for successful lying. However, by the age of four or five years many find lying a useful strategy for avoiding punishment. This early success encourages all of us to continue lying from time to time through adolescence and into adulthood. Let's face it, if you're late for work it is often far simpler to lie and blame the traffic than to admit that you had a hangover and overslept. You may even detect a small sigh of relief on the part of your boss, who won't have to discipline you after all.

One reason why we continue to lie is that we think we can get away with it – and research suggests that we probably can. Most people (particularly politicians) will be relieved to know that 30 years of psychological research have shown that humans aren't good at detecting lies. One stereotype about liars is that they avert their gaze, shift around a lot and touch their noses or clear their throats more than truth tellers do. This is not true. In general, liars tend to move their arms, fingers and hands less and blink less than people who are telling the truth and their voices become more tense or high-pitched. But it's not easy to recognize these clues; laboratory studies have found that, on average, people spot the liars only 55 per cent of the time (Lock, 2004).

By studying a particular politician over a long period, psychologists can sometimes identify behavioural indicators that provide clues as to whether he or she is telling the truth or not. According to Peter Collett (as reported by Leadbeater, 2006), Tony Blair unconsciously fiddles with his little finger when anxious. Bill Clinton bites his upper lip when stressed – and famously did this 15 times when confessing his relationship with Monica Lewinsky.

Whether we spot these tell-tale signs or not, we all know that politicians do lie – or at the very least they use distortions, meaningless slogans and doublespeak. Some of this falsity has been exposed by the Centre for Policy Studies (2008), which points out that politicians are constantly 'drawing lines in the sand' (particularly in Iraq). At times when they are doing nothing at all they claim to be 'learning lessons' about and 'giving urgent consideration' to issues on which they are, of course, 'absolutely clear'. Politicians know that these phrases are a load of bunkum but they believe they can get away with them nonetheless.

Do we force politicians to lie by expecting too much of them? I think we do. They're only human, and if they revealed all their infidelities and misdemeanours there would be no room for other news. After all, even John Major – the dullest of British prime ministers, who was said to have run away from the circus to join a troop of accountants – had a secret extramarital affair whilst in government. Telling the truth or apologizing involves a loss of face and this is something that few are willing to do. Another reason why politicians sometimes lie is because they are certain that we don't want to hear the truth. Do we really want to know that the National Health Service is in a mess, the country is bankrupt and our pensions will be worth virtually nothing come retirement? Probably not.

Nevertheless, a little voice inside us may still hanker after real candour. In the 2003 Richard Curtis film *Love Actually*, the British prime minister, played by Hugh Grant, decides to tell the truth about Britain's 'special relationship' with the United States of America. He reports that he thinks the relationship has become sour, that the USA has become a browbeater and that he intends to stand up to it more forcefully in the future. Although this character says only what people already know, he is feted for telling the truth. Tony Blair referred to this episode with, 'I know there's a bit of us that would like me to do a Hugh Grant in *Love Actually* and tell America where to get off ... but there are ruinous consequences to such behaviour'.

I have a feeling that we are now moving towards an acceptance of the fact that politicians lie, perhaps because we know that we all do so ourselves. Unfortunately, politicians are no different from the rest of us and maybe that is just how it should be. In the meantime, I have a foolproof way of detecting when politicians lie: their lips move.

The mad genius

The suggestion that there may be a link between creative genius and madness dates back to the ancient Greeks, who saw creativity and art as products of a mental disorder bestowed on mortals by the gods. The stereotype of the mad genius has endured and is still common. Many well-known creative geniuses were, it seems, touched by madness: there are numerous examples from the 19th century alone, including the artist Vincent van Gogh (pictured here), composer Robert Schumann, poets Byron and Alfred Lord Tennyson, and many more. Are these high-profile exceptions to the rule, or is it true that there is a link between creative genius and mental instability?

One way of examining the possible link between madness and genius is to explore historical data on creative geniuses of the past. This is not always straightforward because there are variations in both the definition of genius and the accuracy of the data available. However, it appears that psychological symptoms are more prevalent amongst creative people than in the general population: in fact, creative people are twice as likely to suffer from a mental disorder (Ellis, 1926). It is also reported that the more creative a person is, the more likely that he or she will experience depression. Artistic geniuses seem to suffer more than scientific geniuses; one analysis reported that 87 per cent of celebrated poets suffer or have suffered from some sort of psychopathology compared to only 28 per cent of celebrated scientists (Ludwig,

1995). Could it be that artistic people use creative expression as an outlet for their feelings, or do their deeply-felt emotions contribute to their creativity?

Post (1994) examined information about the lives of 291 of the most famous creative figures of our time, including politicians, mathematicians, inventors, composers, painters, sculptors, architects, philosophers, historians, economists, poets, novelists and dramatists. Some of these would certainly be considered geniuses: for example, Albert Einstein, Claude Monet, Pablo Picasso and Charles Dickens. Post found a high incidence of mental disorders amongst these people – particularly the writers, who were by far the most likely to suffer from depression and alcoholism. This finding was so marked that Post contended that these ailments are 'causally linked to some kinds of valuable creativity'.

Current psychiatric data on contemporary creative individuals also suggests that a higher rate of psychopathology is found in creative individuals: depression, alcoholism and suicide are the most common indicators (Simonton, 2005). In the 1950s and 1960s, various personality tests were administered to groups of both creative and non-creative people. Creative people were generally found to have higher scores on some of the personality markers that are frequently associated with psychopathology; once again, this was particularly marked for artists rather than scientists (Simonton, 2004). Nevertheless, the scores of highly creative individuals were still well below those of people classified as psychotic. Creative individuals also had higher scores on traits such as independence and non-conformity, which may be important elements in the creative process (Eysenck, 1995).

Creative individuals may be more open than others to

incoming stimuli perceived through the senses. Many of us disregard incoming information that is irrelevant to our own needs through a process called 'latent inhibition'. Researchers have demonstrated that highly creative people have low levels of latent inhibition, suggesting that they pay greater attention to the information that floods in via all their senses. This information may contribute to the creative process, especially if combined with high intelligence and the ability to concentrate on many things at once. Carson *et al.* (2003) argue that low levels of latent inhibition may predispose a person to mental illness under some conditions and creative accomplishment under others. It is easy to see how one could become overwhelmed by all these stimuli, and a sense of 'not being able to see the wood for the trees' can lead to anxiety and feelings of hopelessness. Fortunately, results from the personality measures also show that creative people display some traits that lessen the likelihood of them suffering from psychopathology. Creative individuals tend to score highly on ego strength, divergent thinking, independence and self-sufficiency: because of this, they are usually able to take control of any bizarre thoughts they may have and channel them into the creative process.

Kay Redfield Jamison, a professor of psychiatry at the Johns Hopkins University School of Medicine, Baltimore, argues that highly creative people experience major mood disorders more often than do other groups in the general population. However, the majority of people who show signs of psychopathology are not extraordinarily creative; conversely, the majority of extraordinarily creative people do not show the symptoms of psychopathology. So how might mental illness and creativity be linked? Jamison suggests that some of the milder symptoms of mania are similar to creative thought. Acutely-tuned senses, restlessness, irritability, thought diversity and the ability to associate divergent ideas and thoughts rapidly are all hallmarks of both the creative and the mildly manic. The sheer number of thoughts coming from a manic person's mind make it more likely that some of these will be creative. In laboratory versions of the 'word association' game, it is noticeable that people undergoing a manic episode form far more new associations to presented words than do normal controls. In one study conducted with this group, common word associations fell by 30 per cent and novel word associations increased by 300 per cent. This change in mental processing may well facilitate original thoughts (Jamison, 1993).

Jamison believes that creative people who suffer from bipolar disorder (once known as manic depression) have a 'built-in editing process' that helps them to deal with the excesses experienced during their manic episodes. The depressive periods can help to put into realistic perspective any material produced during the manic phase of the disorder. It may also be the case that creative work helps provide an emotional release from mild depressive episodes. The poet T S Eliot (1888–1965) wrote,

> Poetry is not a turning loose of emotions, but an escape from emotions, it is not the expression of personality, but an escape from personality. But, of course, only those who have personality and emotion know what it means to want to escape from those things.
>
> Eliot, 1919

It seems that Eliot may have been suggesting that under some circumstances psychopathology may aid the creative process. This view was shared by the artist Edvard Munch (1863–1944), who was wary of seeking treatment for his sufferings, believing that his emotional problems were part of both his being and his art. A further possible link between bipolar disorder and creativity was found by researchers at Stanford University who administered personality assessments to children. They found that the children of parents with bipolar disorder scored significantly higher than other children on creativity scales, suggesting that there may be a genetic link between mood disorders and creativity (Simeonova *et al.*, 2005) – although it may also be possible that these parents created a particularly stimulating environment that also had an influence on the children.

In conclusion, then, the evidence does suggest that genius and psychopathology are linked. You don't have to be mad to be a genius but 'madness' may contribute to some artistic endeavours. Vincent van Gogh painted 80 canvases in the last two manic months of his life and the mental pain he suffered made a significant contribution to the depth and resonance of his work. However, there is not enough evidence to suggest that the relationship between genius and psychopathology is direct or measurable or that the two necessarily go hand in hand: few geniuses could be categorized as mad, and the high-profile exceptions do not prove the rule. For the most part, psychopathology impedes almost all behaviour, creative or otherwise.

➡ *See also* The schizophrenic with the split personality; The violent madman.

The old fogey

> A person who has not made his great contribution to science before the age of 30 will never do so.
>
> Albert Einstein
> (Brodetsky, 1942)

When I was 20, I thought 40 was old and past it but now that I'm 40 I know better – and given that people are living so much longer, I like to think of 40 being the new 20. After all, Mick Jagger, pictured here, seems to think of 65 as being the new 20. Nevertheless it is realistic for all of us occasionally to look ahead to our old age and consider our hopes and plans for this time. The old fogey is stereotyped as old-fashioned, out of touch and generally 'past it'. Is this all we have to look forward to, or are there better things in store? The psychoanalyst Erik Erikson (1968), who outlines the physical, emotional and psychological stages that we go through as we progress through life, suggests that in late adulthood people tend to reflect on their earlier years. Whilst some elderly people may feel a sense of waste, regret or embitterment, many are satisfied with what they have achieved.

Most of us expect to experience some physical and mental infirmity in our later years, but this may not necessarily be the case. It is true that many illnesses and ailments are linked to increasing age. However, a more general deterioration is far from inevitable. We often see what we expect to see, both in others and in ourselves. Your younger brother forgets your birthday and you blame it on his busy lifestyle; your elderly mother forgets too, and you blame it on cognitive decline. If at the age of 80 you lose your purse or wallet it doesn't mean that you can no longer be trusted with managing your finances: after all, young people lose things too. It is important not to over-generalize or we will seriously damage our confidence and conclude that because we can no longer accomplish one thing, other activities too are suddenly outside our realm of competence. Attitude remains the most important factor in healthy aging. A positive attitude can compensate for decline in other areas.

One obvious way in which the elderly may be considered 'past it' relates to their capacity to have sex. Whilst women can continue to have sex well into their later years, men may be less fortunate: impotence increases with age, and by the age of 70 years it affects 67 per cent of men. This doesn't merely affect bedroom activity; it can also have detrimental effects on a man's self-esteem and on his relationship with his partner. Of course, it is not only age that affects a man's ability to maintain an erection: anxiety and the fear of poor sexual performance can also compound the problem (Masters and Johnson, 1970).

The 'old fogey' stereotype suggests that older people (of, say, 65 years and over) are unlikely to want to acquire new skills and may be incapable of doing so. It is true that older people find it difficult to learn new motor skills: the more difficult and demanding the task, the more marked the deficit in learning capacity. This may be because, with age, the brain loses its capacity to process information quickly (Cunningham and Brookbank, 1988). Older people also forget new material more quickly than younger people, but this seems to be a function of poorer initial learning rather than a problem of forgetting per se. With most forms of learning in older people, however, learning still occurs but at a slower rate. Researchers have investigated ways in which the cognitive decline that accompanies aging might be slowed down. Beagles fed a special mix of vitamins and minerals and also kept in a mentally stimulating environment showed a significantly slower cognitive decline than those who were given the enriched diet only (Milgram *et al.*, 2005). Since the neuroanatomy of dogs is comparable to ours, these findings might well be of relevance to humans too: as well as eating healthily, it may be that we need to do a crossword each day in order to be able to continue learning well into our old age.

So much for learning capacity – what about motivation? The hypothesis that older people might be less motivated to learn than their younger friends is not supported by laboratory studies, where they appear just as keen to do well. The eagerness of the elderly to embrace new learning in the field of information technology suggests that this may also be the case in real life. Whilst many studies have found that older people initially have a negative attitude to computers, increasing numbers of 'silver surfers' are now surfing the internet successfully. Given time, training, motivation and a positive attitude, new technology lies well within their grasp (Kelley and Charness, 1995).

In some aspects of life, it may be that men are likely to decline more quickly than women. The 'age–crime curve' shows that most crimes and risk-taking behaviours are committed by people aged between 16 and 22 years. There is also an 'age–genius curve', which shows that productivity fades with age: exceptional men whose brilliance waned in later life include Paul McCartney, J D Salinger, Orson Welles and James Watson. When Kanazawa (2003) looked at the lives of 280 scientists, recording the age at which they made their most useful contribution to scientific knowledge, he found that 65 per cent had peaked before their mid-thirties. He noted a similar age–productivity relationship in jazz musicians, painters, authors and criminals. Kanazawa contends that productivity is a function of two components: genius and effort. Whereas genius does not necessarily decline with age, effort invariably does: Paul McCartney might still be capable of writing another 'Yesterday', but with his place in music history assured and an estimated £200 million already in the bank, he may not have the necessary motivation to do so.

It may be that neither crime nor genius feature in your life history; however, the more general point about effort and productivity is of direct relevance to all of us. The evolutionary reason for the decline in male productivity over time is that both crime and genius are manifestations of a young man's competitive desire to gain a mate and thus increase his chances of reproductive success. A man who does not favour criminal activity can express himself and gain resources through his creative activities instead – and it is by these displays that women may judge his genetic quality; a woman's choice of a mate is strongly influenced by male productivity. The passing years and certain life events in particular (including marriage, the birth of a child and an increase in possessions) cause a noticeable decrease in a man's productivity. This is because the man then devotes more energy and resources to protecting and investing in these new additions to his world – and also because he has all that he needs and seeking more is therefore unnecessary. The good news is that the age–genius curve is less evident in women: older women can still cut the mustard when their menfolk have lost all enthusiasm.

Older people are certainly not past it; they simply need to expend a little more time and effort than they might have done 20 years previously. If you are of a certain age, it's true that you may need to modify your lifestyle where appropriate – but you should try to maintain a realistic perspective, because a positive attitude is all-important. When you can no longer drive, this doesn't mean that you are trapped in your own home – you can take the bus or a taxi instead. Separate the reality from the myths and don't believe the 'old fogey' stereotype. Remember: the benefits of experience usually compensate for any decline.

The main problem that you may need to overcome as you get older is the ageism that is endemic in the West. Made redundant at 55? Western society tells you that you're past your prime and pushes you into early retirement. However, retirement is no longer viewed as the point at which you retreat to your armchair and await the Grim Reaper. On the contrary, it gives you the opportunity to take the 'gap year' that you never had and go backpacking round the world, secure in the knowledge that your final salary pension scheme guarantees you an income for the rest of your life. Failing that, you could retire to Alice Springs: the Aboriginal people, like the Chinese, regard the elderly as repositories of tradition and wisdom. There you will be treated with the respect that you deserve.

➡ *See also* The gold-digging woman and the looks-obsessed man.

The passionate redhead

Two sailors on shore leave are walking down the street when they spot a beautiful blonde. The first sailor asks his friend, 'Have you ever slept with a blonde?' The second sailor says, 'Yes.' They walk a bit further and see a stunning brunette walking towards them. The first sailor asks the other sailor, 'Well, have you ever slept with a brunette?' The second sailor nods, 'Of course, I've slept with brunettes on several occasions.' They continue walking and eye a gorgeous redhead crossing the street. The first sailor asks, 'Well then, have you ever slept with a redhead?' His friend looks at him, smiles and replies, 'Not a wink!'

Jokes about hair colour abound and blondes probably get the worst press of all – at least in the UK. However, there are also negative stereotypes concerning redheads, who are frequently portrayed as passionate in the extreme. A redhead's passion may take the form of a fiery temper or a voracious appetite for sex. The highly-sexed stereotype is usually ascribed to women only: red-headed men are stereotyped as awkward, wimpy and unattractive.

Evidence of the long history of discrimination towards red-headed people may be found in many great works of art, where red hair brings connotations of wilfulness, rapaciousness, rebellion and evil. Michelangelo's fresco on the ceiling of the Sistine Chapel in Rome depicts the fall of Adam and Eve; in this painting, the colour of Eve's hair changes to copper red as soon as she accepts the apple from the (red-headed) serpent. Judas Iscariot, who is said to have betrayed Christ, is often depicted as a redhead – as is the former prostitute Mary Magdalene. Many of the Pre-Raphaelite artists, who flourished in the second half of the 19th century, portrayed ravishing women with red hair (Roach, 2005).

The colour red has always been associated with heat, fire and brimstone and the Devil and to this day it continues to denote strong emotions. Look around the shops just before Valentine's day and you'll almost drown in the sea of red products promoting love and desire. Red as the colour of confrontation and anger also inhabits our everyday world – in expressions such as 'seeing red' or 'red rag to a bull'. Bulls are in fact colour-blind, so red is likely to have no effect on them whatsoever; in humans, however, red has a physiological effect, prompting a measurable increase in blood pressure.

Let's think now about the physiology of red hair – which is caused by two copies of a recessive gene on chromosome 16, and is comparatively rare. On average, between one and two per cent of the world population has red hair, but its incidence is higher in particular areas: four per cent of northern Europeans and 13 per cent of Scots are red-headed (BBC Scotland, 2008). Red-headed criminals will have to be particularly careful in future not to leave traces of DNA at the scene of their crimes. Branicki *et al*. (2007) report that you can tell whether the owner of red-headed DNA has red hair, fair skin and probably hazel or green eyes by looking at genetic variants known as single nucleotide polymorphisms (SNPs). If this fact becomes more widely known, and redheads cease to commit crimes because they know that they will be found out, a new stereotype may suggest that they are the most honest members of society. The physiological distinctiveness of redheads does not end with their genes: they are more susceptible to the effects of strong sunlight and it may be that their pain thresholds are different too. Some researchers claim that redheads require up to 20 per cent more anaesthesia during medical procedures (Liem *et al.*, 2005); others suggest that female redheads are more responsive to certain analgesics (Mogil *et al.*, 2005). Perhaps these conflicting reports support the stereotype that redheads are stubborn and awkward.

To my knowledge, no one has as yet researched the 'hot-tempered redhead' stereotype and I suspect that this is pure myth, probably originating from the visual associations with fire and heat. The Romans may have helped perpetuate this by describing the Picts (an ancient red-headed race from Scotland) as fearsome warriors. Whatever the origins of the stereotype, redheads probably have to suffer more bullying and offensive comments than most, so may be entitled to the occasional angry outburst – another example, perhaps, of the 'self-fulfilling prophecy', which causes us to ignore normal behaviours and focus only on those that confirm our prejudices.

The origins of the 'redheads love sex' stereotype are less obvious; however, there does seem to be some evidence supporting its validity. Hamburg sex researcher Werner Habermehl looked at the sex lives of hundreds of German women in the light of their hair colour. He concluded in an interview with the *Daily Mail* (2006) that

> the sex lives of women with red hair were clearly more active than those with other hair colour, with more partners and having sex more often than the average. The research shows that the fiery redhead certainly lives up to her reputation.
>
> *Daily Mail*, 2006

Habermehl also suggested that, given the well-known redhead stereotype, women who dye their hair red may be signalling to men that they are looking for a partner. However, a redhead who reports more sexual activity may not necessarily behave any differently from other women; it may be simply that men assume that the 'highly sexed' stereotype is true and so this stereotype too acts as a self-fulfilling prophecy. Evidence to support this assertion was reported by Weir and Fine-Davis (1989), who tested the validity of the 'dumb blonde' and 'hot-tempered redhead' stereotypes. Men shown pictures of blondes, redheads and brunettes rated the blondes as less intelligent and the redheads as more temperamental than either blondes or brunettes. This suggests that men buy into both stereotypes.

There is no doubt that a considerable amount of prejudice is directed toward redheads. Labels such as 'carrot top' (though these are actually green), 'copper top' and 'ginger' are frequently used disparagingly – particularly in the UK – and hair colour may even affect the extent to which a person is valued in the workplace. Following a survey that looked at the hair colour of chief executives of the top 500 companies on the London Financial Times Stock Exchange (FTSE), Takeda *et al.* (2006) concluded that if you want to get to the top, the safest bet is to become a brunette. But redheads can also make an impact: for every Judas Iscariot there is a Churchill and for every Henry VIII an Elizabeth I.

➡ *See also* The dumb blonde; The gentleman who prefers blondes; The stressed-out grey-haired person.

The porn-obsessed man

In a popular US sitcom, two of the male characters chance on an unscrambled porn channel and decide not to turn off the TV lest they lose it. It makes great entertainment to watch them trying to ensure that no one (a) turns over to another channel or (b) watches the TV and thus reveals their secret. The scriptwriters are playing on the stereotype that it's men who are obsessed with porn. The female characters wouldn't have reacted in the same way at all: it's more likely that they would have gasped and blanched with shock. This scenario may ring true to *Friends* viewers (for addicts, this is episode 17, fourth season, 'The one with the free porn') – but is it also true to life? If so, what is it about men that makes them behave in this way?

It's not my purpose here to pontificate on the rights and wrongs of pornography but to look at the stereotype that more men than women find it arousing. Pornography is both a serious business and a growth industry: an estimated 33 per cent of internet users in the UK now access the hard-core variety (BBC, 2007). In Sweden, one study suggests that 69 per cent of men and 20 per cent of women use pornography (Cooper *et al.*, 2003) – but perhaps this just reflects a Swedish stereotype. In the US, the pornography industry brings in up to $15 billion (£8.9 billion) annually – more money than the rest of the performing arts combined. More than 10,000 hardcore pornographic films are made in Los Angeles each year, whilst Hollywood – its suburb that is world-famous for mainstream cinematography – makes a total of only 400 movies annually (Marriott, 2003).

Research seems to support the stereotype that more men than women are interested in porn. A study amongst US university students aged between 18 and 26 years found that nearly nine out of ten young men (87 per cent) and nearly one-third (31 per cent) of young women reported using pornography (Carrol *et al.*, 2008). It seems that women are gradually being drawn to porn – possibly because our society is becoming increasingly liberal and permissive. Linda Williams, a US professor of film studies, claimed in 1990 that 40 per cent of US women watched porn videos (Williams, 1990). However, many top-shelf titles are targeted exclusively at the male heterosexual and despite an awareness of the widespread contempt for porn men nevertheless admit that they are aroused by it.

Although neither magazine publishing nor the internet existed millions of years ago, evolutionary psychology is still able to offer some plausible explanations as to why men, rather than women, might be particularly aroused by pornography. First, the fact that a man can become immediately aroused by the sight of a naked woman makes good sense in terms of sexual strategies theory. Any ancestral man who was not aroused in this way would have missed the opportunity to reproduce, have offspring and thus pass on his genes; being aroused by pornographic images may simply be a modern application of this male adaptation.

A second explanation, related to the first, suggests that males are biologically programmed to spread their seed – and the more often this can be done the better. In ancient hunter-gatherer societies, the men who sought the most sexual variety had the greatest chance of passing on their genes. Many male animals, including men, become aroused when watching others copulating. This could prove advantageous to a male who is strong enough to force the other male off or sneaky enough to wait until he leaves; the interloper then takes over while the female is still 'in the mood'. Freshwater male prawns who are not particularly strong or dominant use this cheeky method (Ra'Anan and Sagi, 1985). Perhaps men's arousal at the sight of other people copulating dates from a time when this was a human strategy too, back in our evolutionary past.

A third explanation is psychoanalytic rather than evolutionary. Men's interest in porn may relate to its emphasis on male supremacy. The men portrayed provide visual proof of phallic potency, which may help to reassure men and to allay their fears of impotence.

From a woman's perspective, porn is far less attractive. Women's evolutionary legacy encourages them to invest heavily in their young. Therefore their sexual strategy usually involves attracting a mate who can acquire the resources needed and is willing to commit to a longer-term relationship (Buss, 1998). Research suggests that women are less likely to view positively, use, or be aroused by pornography (Greenberg *et al.* 1993; Malamuth, 1996). These findings fit well with the theory that pornography concentrating on sexual activity without emotional involvement does not fit the female sexual strategy. Another theory – though one that seems to have rather less truth behind it – is that men are more turned on by what they *see* whereas women are more responsive to *sound* (for example, soft music and French accents), mental stimulation and/or romance. This does not seem to be borne out by the research: women appear to be as physically aroused as men by explicit visual stimuli. However, physical arousal is not the only factor that is important to women; whilst they may be physically aroused by some porn, this may be in conflict with their belief that it objectifies and degrades women (Kukkonen, 2007).

So there you have it: women do not use porn as much as men and for this there are various explanations – many of them evolutionary. Well no, not quite. Firstly, there is a problem with evolutionary psychology. It can explain everything yet prove nothing because there is little objective data available; therefore many of the ideas outlined above are controversial. There is no fossil record for complex human behaviours such as sexual attraction, desire and arousal; evolutionary psychology is based on inference, and our hypotheses may be wrong. Furthermore, some suggest that male-dominated societies are all too willing to adhere to evolutionary perspectives that may give scientific justification to men's sexual proclivities. Such societies vary their attitudes to promiscuity depending on the sex of the person involved: a promiscuous man is idolized as a stud; a promiscuous woman is denigrated as a slut.

There is a second uncertainty, which arises from the principal method by which we collect data: self-report. Many believe that women are less likely than men to report their true sexual desires using this method. This point is borne out by the research of Ohio State University psychologist Terri Fisher, who asked men and women whether they masturbated and whether they watched soft- or hard-core pornography; each 'yes' got a point. She found, on average, that men scored 2.32 and women 0.89. She then changed the method of data collection so that respondents were guaranteed anonymity. The women's scores increased to 2.04

whereas the men's scores remained the same. This suggests that the men were less concerned than the women about revealing the details of their sexual activities.

Tuuli Kukkonen of McGill University Health Centre conducted a study that used thermal imaging rather than self-report to measure sexual arousal (Kukkonen *et al.*, 2007). Kukkonen focused thermal imaging cameras on the male and female participants' genitals whilst they watched clips from different films – varying from pornography (experimental condition) to slapstick-style comedy (*The Best of Mr Bean*) and Canadian travelogues (control condition). Most other studies of this sort have required participants to wear measuring instruments that require genital contact, and it has been suggested this may have influenced the types of participants willing to volunteer. Kukkonen's method, although still subject to some methodological concerns, was less likely to be affected by such problems. As the subjects responded to the different films, Kukkonen used a computer in another room to monitor changes in their body temperature – to within one-hundredth of a degree. Both the men and the women began showing arousal within 30 seconds: the men reached maximal arousal in 664.6 seconds, the women in 743 seconds – a statistically negligible difference. In this study, men and women were equally aroused by pornography, and at the same speed. No revealing data was available on their comparative responses to *The Best of Mr Bean* or the Canadian travelogue ...

It does seem that men, rather than women, are the principal consumers of porn – and there are many possible reasons why this may be the case. However, this state of affairs may simply reflect the fact that the porn industry is targeted at men, not women. Perhaps the more important issue for us each to consider personally is what we decide to do with our natural desires for titillation. By the end of the *Friends* episode that I described to you earlier, Chandler finds himself fantasizing about pornographic scenes in every situation he encounters and so tells Joey that they have to stop watching the porn.

➡ *See also* The dirty old man; The gold-digging woman and the looks-obsessed man; The sex-obsessed man; The sower of wild oats.

The promiscuous
gay man

I magine for a moment that you are Dafydd, in the BBC TV comedy show *Little Britain*. As the only gay in Llanddewi-Brefi, you rarely meet any other gay men. So you're almost certainly rather less

promiscuous than the other men in the village. Is *Little Britain* in this respect a microcosm of the whole of the UK? Are all gay men like Dafydd? Of course not. It's just a comedy – insubstantial icing on the cake of real life – and humour often relies on stereotypes as a source of mirth.

The sexual behaviour of gay men and women is an extremely controversial research area. One problem concerning research in this area is common to all studies of human sexual behaviour: much of it is based on people's own accounts – and they do not always tell the truth. The other difficulty is that a surprising amount of the research is accused of being biased (pro-gay or anti-gay) and those involved in the debate that it generates are often criticized for taking either a political or a religious stance. It is not the purpose of this book to push any particular political view. Instead, I shall simply put forward two contrasting arguments that relate to this stereotype. Then you can decide for yourself whether either of them rings true.

The first hypothesis suggests that gay men could be more promiscuous than straight men and that there may be some reasons for this. Symons (1979) proposed that sexual orientation mediates certain mating behaviours and preferences in humans. Research generally supports the stereotype that men go for looks in a partner; they also tend to show more interest in casual sex. Symons tentatively suggested that such preferences could be even more exaggerated in gay men (and lesbians) compared to straight men (and women). In straight relationships, each partner has to make compromises in order to accommodate the sexual style of the other sex. In gay relationships, Symons suggested, both partners are given free rein to express themselves however they may wish.

Bailey *et al.* (1994) claimed to have collected some data indicating that gay men were more likely than heterosexual men to have many partners and to indulge in casual sex. Heterosexual men showed just as much *interest* in short-term relationships, but were less likely to follow this through by actually engaging in them. Neither homosexual nor heterosexual men were interested in potential partners' employment status or earnings; however, both were very interested in potential partners' physical attractiveness and in visual sexual stimuli in general. So it seems that homosexual and heterosexual men have similar attitudes to sex, but heterosexual men's behaviours may be curbed by the expectations of their female partners. This may suggest, in theory at least, that gay men are likely to be more promiscuous than heterosexual men.

The second hypothesis suggests that straight men might be more promiscuous than gay men, and some data is available to support this alternative view. Fay (1989), in a study involving both gay and bisexual men, found that 24 per cent had one male sexual partner in their lifetime, 45 per cent had between two and four, 13 per cent had between five and nine, and 18 per cent had ten or more. These statistics produce a mean average of six sexual partners per man. A similar study conducted by Billy *et al.* (1993)

– mainly among straight men – produced a mean average of 7.3 partners. This suggests that gay men tend to have fewer sexual partners than heterosexual men.

Another couple of studies support this finding. Binson *et al.* (1995), working with a sample of 2,664 gay participants, found that gay men reported an average of 6.5 sexual partners in the last five years. In a parallel study looking at data over one year, Dolcini *et al.* (1993) reported that heterosexual men were less likely to be celibate than homosexual or bisexual men. The table below compares the results of these two research projects, giving the percentage of men and their reported numbers of sexual partners.

Sexual orientation	No partners	One partner	Two or more partners	Data source
Gay	24%	41%	35 %	Binson *et al.*, 1995
Straight	8%	80%	12%	Dolcini *et al.*, 1993

A third study, and one which is generally seen as comprehensive and methodologically sound, was conducted by Laumann *et al.* (1994). They found that the median (middle) number of sexual partners for heterosexuals in their study was five and for homosexuals six. However, the researchers suggested that the mean was unduly influenced by a small subpopulation of gay males who tended towards high rates of sexual partners. They concluded that the difference in numbers of partners was not significantly different and that:

the higher mean numbers of partners for respondents
reporting same-gender sex corresponds to a stereotype
of male homosexuals that is widespread in our society.
While some evidence in our data supports this general
tendency, the differences do not appear large, in view of
the higher variability in our measures that results from
the small sample size of homosexually active men.

Laumann *et al.*, 1994

One other study of note is the General Social Survey (GSS)
published by the University of Chicago, which is widely regarded
as one of the single best sources of data on societal trends from
1972 to the present day. The statistics for the period 1972 to 2002
suggest that gay and straight men have about the same number
of sexual partners. The only discrepancy occurred with a small
number of gay men (about ten per cent) who reported high levels
of promiscuity, with between 20 and 100 or more than 100 partners
in a given five-year period. Perhaps a fair conclusion from this
data would be that almost 90 per cent of gay men display the
same levels of promiscuity as unmarried straight men (Fisher,
2006).

The real truth is that we do not have completely reliable
information about anybody's sexual behaviour – and even if we
did, where would this lead us? Even if the average gay man were
shown to be promiscuous, and the evidence does not support
this, we could not conclude that being gay leads to promiscuity
or that any particular gay person is promiscuous. Whilst a small
proportion of gay men might be considered more promiscuous
than others, there are heterosexuals who could be labelled in
exactly the same way – and we cannot ignore heterosexual

promiscuity whilst negatively stereotyping the same behaviour in homosexuals. The vast majority of homosexuals seem to have fewer sexual partners on average than heterosexuals. So it seems unfair and also incorrect to label all homosexuals as more promiscuous than all heterosexuals.

➡ *See also* The dirty old man; The gold-digging woman and the looks-obsessed man; The sex-obsessed man; The sower of wild oats.

The sadistic prison guard

The stereotype is that the torturer ... is driven by a warped sadism. But more commonly, some psychologists say, torturers are often not sadists so much as otherwise normal people who under certain circumstances sink into a routine of intimate horror in which they hurt or mutilate another human being, while staying aloof from the screams and agony of their victims.

Goleman, 1985

It is comforting to think that people who torture others might be sadists because this attitude allows us to view them as a race apart – unrelated to the people we encounter on a day-to-day basis. When prisoners are grossly maltreated, as they are from time to time around the world, we may zealously protect our carefully constructed comfort zone, placing the blame on a few 'bad apples' who are 'evil'. We reassure ourselves that such depravity is rare and will only occur when a small minority find themselves in particular situations – and perhaps there is something about the prison guard role that attracts people with sadistic tendencies. Here I want to consider an alarming but possible alternative: that we may all have an inherent dark side that could make us capable of abuse.

In 1963, the US social psychologist Stanley Milgram (1933–84) conducted an experiment that investigated the concept of obedience to authority. He invited each participant into the laboratory under the pretence that he or she was going to take part in a study on memory. A confederate of Milgram's pretended to be the 'learner' and was wired up to an electric chair in another room. The participant was then asked to administer to the learner increasingly powerful electric shocks (up to 450 volts)

....

as punishment for answering questions incorrectly. In response, the confederate would scream in agony, ask to be let out, kick the wall and finally, at 315 volts, stop responding altogether. Although only fake shocks were given, the participant was unaware of this during the experiment. The researchers believed that only a few participants – those who might show sadistic tendencies – would obey the orders and administer any shocks at all. Much to their surprise, they were quite wrong: 65 per cent of participants obeyed all the orders given and gave electric shocks up to the maximum level of 450 volts (which, if genuine, would have been fatal). They continued to do so even after the 'learner' had become unresponsive. This was the first study to suggest that people sometimes behave not as a result of 'dispositional' or personality factors, but because of the situations in which they find themselves (Milgram, 1963).

Eight years later, Philip Zimbardo conducted a study into the effect a prison environment can have on both guards and prisoners. Zimbardo and his colleagues (Haney *et al.*, 1973) created a simulated prison in the basement of Stanford University's psychology department. They recruited 24 emotionally stable male participants, half of whom were randomly assigned to the role of 'guards'; the others became 'prisoners'. On arrival at the prison, each prisoner was stripped naked and had a chain bolted around one ankle. He was also issued with a loose-fitting smock showing his identity number on the front and back, and was referred to only by this number. The guards wore military-style khaki uniforms and silver reflector sunglasses that made eye contact impossible; they carried clubs, whistles, handcuffs and keys. The guards had almost complete control over the prisoners, who were locked in their cells around the clock – except for meals, toilet privileges, headcounts and work.

Although all the participants were fully aware that this was only a simulation, the guards quickly created a brutal atmosphere. The prison experiment was supposed to last two weeks but within five days things were spinning out of control. As the guards stepped up their aggression, the prisoners began to feel increasingly helpless. Every guard behaved in an abusive, sadistic, authoritarian way at some point and many seemed to revel in their new-found power, devising new ways in which to humiliate their victims. So severe was some of the guards' abuse that the prisoners began to show signs of severe stress, anxiety and depression. The experiment was stopped. Zimbardo concluded that the participants, who had been selected as psychologically healthy and 'normal', had been transformed into behaving sadistically by the demands of the situation.

Later, Zimbardo (2004) outlined the ten conditions that he believes may prompt an ordinary individual to behave in an evil way.

- Create an ideology where the ends justify the means.
- Get participants to agree to comply with the situation.
- Give participants meaningful roles with clear social values.
- Ensure that the rules of expected behaviour are vague.
- Label the actors and actions in a negative way (for example, use the term 'enemies' rather than 'people').
- Ensure that participants do not feel entirely responsible for their actions. Providing a level of anonymity (for example, blindfolding prisoners or making all the guards look the same) will contribute to this.

- Make small requests initially and increase the demands gradually.
- Initially, make the leader seem compassionate.
- Allow verbal dissent provided that the compliance continues.
- Make it difficult for participants to leave the situation.

Adapted from Zimbardo, 2004

Many of these rules are applied in a variety of prison situations around the world; the more firmly they take hold, the greater the risk that evil acts may be carried out.

Zimbardo summarizes what he learned from his research as follows: 'virtually anyone could be recruited to engage in evil deeds that deprive other human beings of their dignity, humanity and life' (Zimbardo, 2004). Some psychologists believe that Zimbardo's interpretation overemphasizes the situational explanation. It is possible that the behaviour of the participants may have been influenced by their stereotyped expectations of how prisoners and guards 'should' behave: after all, they were only role-playing. In response, Zimbardo contends that the participants believed in the reality of the situation and that the powerful situational influences would be even more powerful in a real prison with convicted prisoners.

The depressing conclusion is that prison guards may not be any more sadistic than the rest of us – on the contrary, everyone is capable of committing acts of brutality in certain circumstances. However, not all Zimbardo's guards acted in the same sadistic way; there were marked differences between them – at least some of which were determined by their different personalities. An 'integrated theory' of human behaviour suggests that how people behave is determined not only by the demands of the situations in which they find themselves, but by a complex interplay of these demands with facets of their individual personality and sociocultural background. History shows that when individuals are placed in situations that demand them to behave in an evil and brutal way they are sometimes strong enough to resist – and can encourage others to do so as well. We are not merely puppets, manipulated by the demands of a particular situation. Being aware of the dangers of situational demands can go a long way to negating their insidious effects and this awareness should allow all of us to take personal responsibility for what we do.

We must all remain aware of our potential to act sadistically – as bullies in the playground or workplace if not as prison guards. That doesn't mean that, given the wrong circumstances, evil will be the inevitable result. When it comes to institutionalized violence and torture it's not so much a case of a few bad apples – it may instead be the barrel that taints us all (Zimbardo, 2008).

The schizophrenic with the split personality

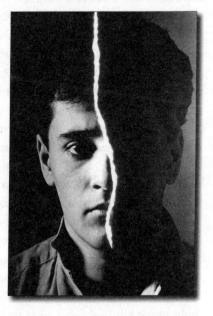

Perhaps the most common of all the many popular misconceptions concerning schizophrenia is that people with this condition have multiple personalities. A Harris Poll conducted for the National Organization on Disability in the USA reported that about 66 per cent of those surveyed believed 'split personality' to be a key characteristic of the disorder (ABC Science Online, 2004).

This is definitely not the case – and a schizophrenic is not a person 'torn in two'. The earliest name for schizophrenia was 'dementia praecox', meaning 'early-onset dementia'. Emil Kraepelin (1856–1926), who is seen by some as the founder of modern psychiatry, used this name to describe a degenerative illness that impaired intellectual functioning. The term 'schizophrenia' was coined later, in 1911, by the Swiss psychiatrist and psychologist Eugen Bleuler (1857–1939); it comes from the Greek words meaning 'split' and 'mind'. This is where the confusion arises: schizophrenia means 'split mind' rather than 'split personality'. 'Split mind' alludes to the fact that people with schizophrenia are separated from reality to such an extent that they have difficulty distinguishing between the real and the unreal. Whilst a person with this condition has a single personality, his or her split mind may have two distinct trains of thought running simultaneously. One train of thought may cut across the other with insulting language or 'bad' thoughts; sometimes it provides a running commentary (often negative) on what the person is doing. It is estimated that about one in every 100 people will develop schizophrenia at some point in their life (American Psychiatric Association, 1994). Today there are estimated to be about 500,000 people in the UK suffering from this illness.

It is commonly accepted that there are three types of schizophrenia. The first, which accounts for the majority of cases, is paranoid schizophrenia. People with this illness often believe that they are being persecuted or watched by a whole range of people – including their neighbours and even the police. They tend to be easily agitated, argumentative and angry. Secondly there is catatonic schizophrenia, which compels the sufferer to hold his or her limbs in a rigid position for hours on end. People with this kind of schizophrenia often show extreme negativism, and will tend to do the opposite of what is asked of them. Thirdly, there is disorganized or hebephrenic schizophrenia, characterized by inappropriate moods and disorganized and incoherent speech that is difficult to understand.

The key symptoms of schizophrenia can be split into two groups: positive and negative. Positive symptoms are bizarre additions to ordinary behaviour, such as delusions, paranoia and hallucinations. The most common hallucination is 'hearing voices' and this is experienced by most people suffering from any of the different types of schizophrenia. People with negative symptoms lack some of the day-to-day behaviours that we take for granted. As a result they have 'flat' emotions, are underactive, speak little (and use a limited vocabulary), lack enjoyment of life and are indifferent to their own appearance or safety.

The 'split personality' myth is not the only common misconception concerning schizophrenia. First, there is a belief that the condition may be caused by bad parenting. When researchers were unable to find an obvious biological explanation for the illness, the spotlighted shifted to possible problems within the person's family relationships. As a result, the term 'schizophrenogenic mother' was coined to describe a cold, dominant and conflict-inducing parent (Gross and Rolls, 2006). Nowadays the weight of evidence supports a biological cause for schizophrenia, operating in conjunction with certain environmental triggers – which, as yet, are poorly understood. Another misconception is that people with schizophrenia are unstable and possibly violent. This is completely unfounded: statistics show that people with schizophrenia are no more likely to commit violent crimes than others in the general population, although they are more likely to be victims of crime.

One reason why there seem to be so many incorrect beliefs about schizophrenia is that the popular media often present the illness in an extremely negative light. Hollywood confuses schizophrenia with 'multiple personality disorder' – or 'dissociative identity disorder', as it is now more commonly known. Neither the knife-wielding Norman Bates in Alfred Hitchcock's *Psycho* (1960) nor Jim Carrey in *Me, Myself and Irene* (Bob and Peter Farrelly, 2000) show the true symptoms of schizophrenia. In fact, many mental health professionals were so incensed by the inaccurate portrayal of the condition in *Me, Myself and Irene* that they made a protest against it (Baron-Faust, 2000). However, Ron Howard's Oscar®-winning film *A Beautiful Mind* (2001), starring Russell Crowe, gained plaudits from the critics and the mental health community alike. In this biography of the mathematical genius John Nash, the effects of the negative symptoms that he experienced are portrayed particularly accurately and sensitively (Smith and Cooper, 2006).

Some academics, such as Paul Hammersley of the University of Manchester, believe that the term schizophrenia should be abolished, laying to rest at last the inaccurate stereotypes that are associated with this debilitating mental illness (BBC News, 2006). The Campaign to Abolish the Schizophrenia Label (CASL) advocates the use of a new name, such as 'dopamine dysregulation' or 'neurobiological disease', thus leaving behind the incorrect stereotypes and negative connotations associated with the current terminology. Despite the lobby for change, however, the term schizophrenia is likely to remain in use for the time being: given the wide range of symptoms that a new umbrella term would need to cover, health professionals are finding it hard to agree on a suitable alternative.

I'm all for the renaming of schizophrenia, but we need to bear in mind that this strategy may not necessarily have the desired effect. Chung and Chan (2004) investigated the effect that re-translating the term schizophrenia would have on adolescent schoolchildren living in Hong Kong; disappointingly, it had no effect at all. On the positive side, however, the level of stigma held by this young sample before the change in terminology was not as high as the authors had anticipated. Maybe this indicates that some of the misconceptions about the illness have not been handed down to the next generation. Meanwhile, perhaps the groundswell of opinion that seeks to promote a more accurate understanding of the condition should turn its attention to Hollywood. The realistic portrayal of mental illness in a blockbuster film is more likely to educate the public than volumes of academic papers, however carefully they may have been researched.

➡ *See also* The mad genius; The violent madman.

The sex-obsessed man

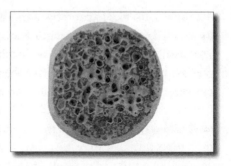

It's a commonly held belief that men are so obsessed by sex that they think about it at least once every seven seconds. No one knows where this statistic originated but it's quoted so often that many now believe it to be true.

I've often wondered why it is that I only think about sex every eight or nine seconds ... For this reason it comes as quite a relief to find that research does not back up this oft-reported statistic. Research conducted by the Kinsey Institute, Indiana University, suggests that just over 50 per cent of men think about sex at least once every day, with 43 per cent of men doing so a few times per week and four per cent only once a month or less. Of course, there are some men who think about sex several times per day, but every seven seconds seems a bit extreme.

Leitenberg and Henning (1995) report various studies that demonstrate clear differences between the sexes in this respect. Research by Cameron (1967) involved asking 103 male participants and 130 female participants to estimate the percentage of time that they thought about sex. As many as 55 per cent of men and 42 per cent of women reported that they thought of sex more than ten per cent of the time. A few years later, Cameron and Biber (1973) conducted a large-scale survey of the frequency of sexual thoughts with over 4,400 individuals across a number of age ranges. In order to ascertain whether they'd had a sexual thought in the last five minutes, they asked the question, 'Did you think about sex or were your thoughts sexually coloured even for a moment in the last five minutes?' (What colour would that be, incidentally? Maybe purple, or blue?) In the age range 14 to 25 years, 52 per cent of men and 39 per cent of females replied in the affirmative. In the age range 26 to 55 years, the figures were 26 per cent for men and 14 per cent for women. In a review of sexuality conducted in 1994, involving 3,342 men and women, Laumann *et al.* (1994) reported a greater gender difference, with 54 per cent of men reporting that they have sexual thoughts at least once a day compared to only 19 per cent of women.

One analysis – from a book by Louann Brizendine, a neuropsychiatrist at the University of California (Brizendine, 2006) – has hit the headlines. In *The Female Brain*, Brizendine claims that the brains of men, when compared to the brains of women, have twice as much space and processing power devoted to sex. This assertion is fundamental to Brizendine's claim that 85 per cent of men aged between 20 and 30 years think about sex every 52 seconds, whereas women think about it only once a day. Mark Liberman (2006) tracked down the references quoted by Brizendine, and concluded that the best evidence was reported by Jones and Barlow (1990). In this study, just under 100 male and female undergraduates were asked to keep a week-long diary detailing their sexual fantasies ('internally generated thoughts') and urges ('externally provoked sexual thoughts'). Young heterosexual men reported a greater frequency of sexual urges than did women (men: 4.5 per day; women: 2.0 per day), though the frequency of fantasies was similar for both sexes (2.5 per day). Liberman then did the maths. According to his calculations, men had a total of seven sexual thoughts per day (one thought every 12,342 seconds); women had a sexual thought every 19,200 seconds. On the basis of these figures, Lieberman suggests that

Brizendine's research portrays men as 237 times hornier than can be inferred from the research findings.

In conclusion, the considerable quantity of research into how frequently men and women think about sex suggests that men may think about it slightly more frequently than do women. However, they do not think about it as frequently as every seven seconds, and this certainly does not indicate an obsession. Even the 52 seconds claim appears dubious. But if it helps to sell a book? Now there's an idea …

➡ *See also* The porn-obsessed man; The promiscuous gay man.

The slim and seductive woman

N owadays virtually every catwalk model appears to be a 'size zero': this US dress size, equivalent to a UK size 4, is fast becoming the ideal for many image-conscious women throughout the Western world. Our obsession with extreme slenderness is now a focus for debate in some circles: this demonstrates a concern that young girls who seek to emulate the supermodels may fall prey to eating disorders as a result. But what is the view of the average man in the street? Does he find slim women particularly seductive, or is this just a popular myth?

One well-known measure of attractiveness is a woman's waist–hip ratio (WHR). Numerous studies have shown that the WHR is a reliable measure of attractiveness in women. In a groundbreaking and oft-cited study, Singh (1993) asked participants to rank in order of attractiveness twelve line drawings that represented four levels of WHR at three levels of body weight (underweight, normal, and overweight). He conducted a couple of studies, with male and female participants ranging in age from 18 to 60 years. The woman rated as the most attractive, healthy and suitable for reproduction was of normal weight, with a WHR of 0.7. Similar findings were subsequently found in studies that used photographs rather than line drawings (Singh, 1994).

Singh (1993) proposed 0.7 as the ideal WHR after analysing the WHR for *Playboy* centrefolds and winners of the Miss America contests. A few years later, Freese and Meland (2002) revisited this data, and found the median WHR to be 0.676. The robust relationship that exists between attractiveness and WHR may arise from an association between curviness and fertility. A woman with a WHR that is close to the ideal measure has an 'hourglass figure' – shapely breasts and broad hips set against a narrow waist. A WHR that is significantly higher or lower than the ideal may give warning signals of poor reproductive capabilities and a high risk of disease. A high WHR may also give the appearance of pregnancy – thereby warning a male suitor that he may, for the time being, have missed an opportunity for the woman to bear his offspring.

A woman's WHR is known to relate directly to the levels of oestrogen and testosterone in her body: as oestrogen decreases and testosterone increases, so too does the WHR increase (Singh, 1993). Women with lower WHRs (and hence lower testosterone and higher oestrogen levels) tend to get pregnant more easily – provided that the WHR does not drop too low. High WHRs (and hence higher testosterone and lower oestrogen levels) may be associated with health and fertility problems (Symons, 1995), skin problems including acne (Pearl *et al.*, 1998) and body hair. This collection of traits, generally considered to be unattractive in women, does not bode well for reproductive success. Given such findings, it is likely that as men have evolved they may well have developed the ability to register a woman's WHR (consciously or otherwise) and use it to assess her potential as a mate who will bear children. It is also evident that women have used this knowledge to enhance their attractiveness by emphasizing and advertising their low WHR through particular types of clothing, such as well-tailored garments or even girdles, corsets or bodices.

However, a cross-cultural study has questioned whether a relatively low WHR is attractive to men the world over, or only to those in the West. Wetsman and Marlowe (1999) showed the line drawings used by Singh (1993) to men from the Hadza tribe of Tanzania, who live as foragers and are isolated from Western culture. The Hadza men did not find the WHR of 0.7 particularly attractive, showing a preference for higher ratios. When Yu and Shepard (1998) studied tribal cultures, they found that as the degree of Westernization increased, so did preferences for a low WHR. In their discussion of this finding, they suggest that in close-knit, small-scale tribal societies people have greater first-hand knowledge of potential partners; they are therefore less reliant on physical indicators that may provide clues to the suitability of a mate.

Tovée *et al.* (1999) used real pictures of identically-dressed women, manipulated to show variations in WHR and body mass index (BMI), which is a standard measure of height against weight. They found that small alterations in BMI had a large influence on how attractive the women were seen to be, and that these alterations made more impact than any variations in WHR. As a result, they argued that BMI is the more important factor in determining attractiveness. Swami *et al.* (2007) showed males and females images of real women in five categories, from emaciated to obese, and asked them to rate their attractiveness. The 'normal' BMI range, according to the World Health Organization, is between 18.5 and 25: in Britain, the BMI that was seen as the most attractive was 20.85; in Malaysia, the figure was marginally higher. The British results also showed that attractiveness dropped quickly either side of the 20.85 figure. Although the obese women were rated as only half as attractive as a woman with the optimal BMI figure, the thinner women received even lower ratings.

Yet the 'slim is seductive' stereotype persists. Buss (2003) reports that US women overestimate men's preferences for thinness in women. When asked to choose separately their ideal build and the build most attractive to men, women chose slimmer-than-average figures for both. Men, however, chose figures of average build. Perhaps women are incorrect in their belief that men like their women to be slimmer than average – maybe because they pay too much attention to the images in the media.

In conclusion: whether attractiveness is measured in terms of WHR or BMI, the thinnest women are not necessarily seen as the most attractive. A WHR of 0.7 or a BMI of 20.85 seems the ideal in the West, and studies in other parts of the world suggest that the fuller figure may be preferred. Who's brave enough to tell the celebrities?

➡ *See also* The lazy fatty; The gold-digging woman and the looks-obsessed man.

The slothful student

Everyone knows that students never wash up, never rise before 11am and leave all their essays until the last minute, when they buy them online. The only time they become animated is when they are misappropriating traffic cones

for silly pranks or desperately scrambling for last orders at the bar. Students don't have much money because they don't bother to get jobs to fund their education. The money they do have is all spent in the pub or at the takeaway – they're far too slothful to cook their own meals.

Before I am lynched by a mob of hard-working students who pause between essays to take their revenge, I must assure you that I am only painting the stereotyped picture that will be familiar to many. Of course, by no means all students fit the stereotype. Many of my students, for example, hold down responsible part-time jobs whilst studying at the same time.

Being lazy is viewed as a particularly unattractive trait, since it is regarded as being within the individual's own sphere of control. Accusations of laziness are levelled at every generation as each new set of students is confronted by parents and grandparents who claim to have worked much harder when they were at college. Advances in technology accentuate further the differences between one generation and the next – and as the speed of technological change accelerates, so the differences seem ever greater. These days, even the most conscientious of students may be tempted to laziness: easy access to websites containing lecture notes means that although note-taking in a lecture is a good way of engaging with the material, students don't really need to stir from their beds. Lecturers may make their Microsoft PowerPoint® slides available online – and if they distribute photocopies of key research papers as well, students may not need to visit the library either.

Let's think for a moment about laziness and activity in more general terms, and what factors may have influenced these behaviours in humans. Looking back to our evolutionary past, we had to keep active in order to survive. When we were thirsty we found water, when we were hungry we went hunting: we had to meet the constant demands of survival. Being lazy meant that you missed your next meal – and if this lazy behaviour were to recur regularly, and you continued missing meals, then you would eventually die. So why hasn't the trait of laziness died out from the gene pool? Because it was also important for early humans to conserve energy whenever possible. We have therefore evolved as creatures who expend minimal energy when circumstances permit.

For this reason, all of us are prone to 'student syndrome', which prevents us from applying ourselves to a task until the deadline is upon us – despite the fact that we are given plenty of time in which to complete it. The syndrome particularly affects students who are asked to write essays within a fixed timeframe but find this impossible. Some generous tutors will allow them extensions, but these are unlikely to help because there are always other tasks whose demands are more immediate: so the same pattern recurs, and again students are unable to apply themselves until the last minute. You can see and experience this same prevarication in many settings, including the filing of tax returns: one year the HM Revenue and Customs website crashed on the last day that returns were due – simply because so many people were filing their returns at the eleventh hour.

Nevertheless there are times when students wholeheartedly apply themselves to their academic work, and to good effect. It is difficult to ascertain exactly the length of time the average student spends on college work: after all, a discussion of Shakespeare might equally well take place in the pub as in a seminar room. However, the Higher Education Policy Institute, following a survey of 15,000 students, has estimated that UK students spend an average of 26 hours per week on their studies. This is somewhat less than students in Germany, who study for about 35 hours a week, and students in Portugal, who pore over their books for an impressive 40 hours (MacLeod, 2007).

One possible reason for laziness is lack of motivation: that is, an unwillingness to initiate or continue with an activity. Psychologists believe that there are six major factors that impact on student motivation – and, in turn, laziness. These are as follows.

- **Attitude**: Students who have a poor attitude to their work are often lazy as a result. However, their attitudes can be improved if they have positive experiences of studying at school or college.
- **Need**: According to Maslow's 'hierarchy of needs' (Maslow, 1943) everyone has similar needs: these include physiological needs (such as hunger and thirst), safety needs (including basic security and protection), social needs (including a sense of belonging and love), self-esteem needs (including recognition and status) and self-actualization needs (which, when met, allow us to become creative, spontaneous people who are able to solve

problems successfully). If students are to achieve some of the 'higher' goals, which will enable them to study and learn effectively, their basic physiological and safety needs must first be met. It is easy to see that they may appear lazy with regard to college work when forced to expend much of their energy on poorly-paid jobs simply to pay for their accommodation and food.

- **Stimulation**: All of us, students included, require stimulation in order to function at our best. Perhaps too many college courses fail to arouse the interests of students, who see them as detached from the real world. A learning environment where students are actively involved in their learning may be one way of helping them to feel fully engaged and committed.
- **Mood**: Mood or 'affect' can influence motivation levels. Many students are adolescents and may be prone to mood swings that have a detrimental effect on their studies.
- **Competence or ability**: A certainty that one is capable of achieving the goal set is another motivational factor that can help to counteract laziness. It is therefore important that students choose courses that are suited to their abilities. The reason why some students cannot complete the task in hand may not be laziness, but the fact that they lack the skills or confidence required. Perhaps some courses are inappropriate to the needs, interests and abilities of our young people.
- **Reinforcement**: There are two types of reinforcement – positive and negative.

  Positive reinforcement involves gaining a reward in recognition of a particular behaviour: for example, being paid for work completed. The reward acknowledges and reinforces the work done – and if the reward is sufficiently valued it is likely that the good behaviour will be repeated. The positive message is strongest when only a short time elapses between the behaviour and the reward. However, the immediate reward for handing in an essay on time may be no more than a fleeting sense of self-satisfaction, followed by a cursory 'Well done' scribbled on the script four weeks later. These small reinforcements will not be enough for many students. To make matters worse, many of them are blind to the fact that more hours of study may result in a better degree and a better job in the future. The prospect of the reward is too distant and the link between time spent studying and future job prospects could be tenuous, since the latter will be influenced by numerous other factors too.

Negative reinforcement occurs when a behaviour is performed only in order to avoid some other undesirable condition. Some students may go to college only to avoid the more unpleasant option of getting a job. Once there, they may stay in bed to avoid the more onerous task of attending lectures. Do students get punished for staying in bed or missing lectures? Probably not – they're more likely nowadays to be offered podcasts of the lectures on their mobile phones.

Many young people have problems with motivation that date from their schooldays. Research has shown that boys are less motivated than girls when it comes to schoolwork – in spite of the fact that they are equally motivated in their social and personal goals. Boys' laziness in relation to schoolwork may be caused by a failure to see the connection between their own behaviour and a measured outcome. In other words, they convince themselves that time spent on revision will not necessarily make a difference to their final grades. Peer pressures also conspire against boys, further dissuading them from putting in the hours of study needed if they are to do well: revising is not cool. This attitude may well continue into the next stage of their education.

Mel Levine, in *The Myth of Laziness* (Levine, 2003), claims that some laziness can be attributed to neurodevelopmental dysfunctions caused by a combination of genetic and environmental factors. Levine is sympathetic to people who display lazy behaviour, believing that just as we do not label people as 'stupid' (although sometimes their *behaviour* might be described as stupid), so we should avoid giving people the unhelpful label 'lazy'. Taking a thoroughly optimistic view, Levine suggests that the emphasis should instead be on creating environments that discourage lazy behaviour – thus reflecting his firm belief that everyone wants to succeed. I agree that most people have a desire to be productive but I'm not convinced that everyone is prepared to put in the effort required.

Students may be lazy on occasions but this is not surprising since their circumstances often conspire to encourage such behaviour: given the opportunity, we are all slothful creatures. If I won the lottery tomorrow, I would have the opportunity to give up work and lead a life of leisure; I would seize this opportunity eagerly – as would most people, I suspect, even if they were to risk being branded lazy. Why? Because the opportunity is there. It's human nature. The reason why some students are lazy is because they can be lazy. Nowadays we have an overabundance of essential resources and thus less motivation to satisfy our immediate needs. People who continue to work hard even when their immediate needs have been met are thinking of future needs and plans. However, many of us find immediate rewards more enticing: hence, the immediate reward of watching TV is far more attractive than going to a lecture that might be of help in a future exam.

I could continue writing, but the book deadline is months away. So I'm going to watch TV instead.

➡ *See also* The lazy fatty.

The sower of wild oats

I've got a mate whose nickname is 'shagger'. You may find that funny but she doesn't like it.

Jimmy Carr, *Live at the Apollo*, BBC 1 (December 2007)

The phrase 'sowing wild oats' is a euphemism for promiscuous behaviour, and is usually indulged in by men. Some men wear their reputation of promiscuity as a badge of honour, whereas most women regard it as shameful; this fact and numerous other examples of the differences between men and women in their attitudes to sex are explored by comedians worldwide. This particular stereotype is perhaps summed up most accurately with the oft-quoted remark, 'Women need a reason to have sex. Men just need a place.' But is it really true that men are more willing than women to indulge in casual sex?

If sex is often a target for humour, it is also the subject of much research – and the research gives overwhelming support to the hypothesis that many men feel that they must sow their 'wild oats' when the opportunity presents itself (Okami and Shackelford, 2001; Clark, 1990). Clark and Hatfield (1989) report two studies in which 96 university students asked volunteers of average attractiveness to approach members of the opposite sex whom they had never met before and ask them one of three questions:

- Would you go out with me tonight?
- Will you come over to my apartment?
- Would you go to bed with me?

Men and women were equally willing to go on a date with a person they'd just met. However, men were eleven times more likely than women to agree to visit the person's apartment. Whilst no women accepted the offer of sex, 75 per cent of the men did. Furthermore, many of the men who turned down the invitation apologized for not being able to accept because they were already in a relationship. None of the women responded apologetically, and this suggests that their refusal was not dependent on any other factor: they were simply not interested. We can safely conclude that, whereas many men find appealing the idea of sex with a stranger, women do not (Buss, 1994).

One possible explanation for women's reticence in this area is that they fear for their physical safety in encounters with male strangers. However, further analysis of related data suggests that this is not the case. Not one woman expressed fears for her safety as a reason for refusing sex with a stranger; furthermore, about 50 per cent of the women were willing to date the stranger, although this too could have placed them in a risky situation. In a later study, Clark (1990) arranged for close friends to inform each participant that a specific person they knew well wanted to have sex with them. Clark's purpose was to assure the women that safety would not be an issue in this case. The women remained uninterested in having sex but were willing to go out with the men. Finally, research by Bailey *et al.* (1994) found that lesbians, who do not run the risk of male-perpetrated violence, display a similar lack of interest in casual sex.

Two studies conducted in the 1990s clearly demonstrate men's interest in sowing wild oats. Buss and Schmitt (1993) asked men and women how likely they would be to have sex with someone they had known for an hour, a day, a week, a month, six months, a year, two years or five years. Only at the five-year measure did they find similar levels of agreement in both sexes. At all other time periods, men were far more likely to agree to have sex. Perhaps more surprising are the responses to the following question, which Ellis and Symons (1990) put to men and women who were married or in a relationship:

> If the opportunity presented itself of having sexual intercourse with an anonymous member of the opposite sex who was as competent a lover as your partner but no more so, and who was as physically attractive as your partner but no more so, and there was no risk of pregnancy, discovery, or disease, and no chance of forming a more durable relationship, do you think you would do so?
>
> Ellis and Symons, 1990

Four times as many men as women answered that they 'certainly would,' and women were two and a half times more likely than men to answer that they 'certainly wouldn't'. Men who were not in a steady relationship were six times more likely than women to answer in the affirmative.

There is a huge weight of further evidence that supports different aspects of this stereotype. For example: the majority of those who visit prostitutes are men (Burley and Symanski, 1981); comparisons of male and female erotica suggest that women put more emphasis on romance (Ellis and Symons, 1990); casual sex leaves women with negative feelings of vulnerability and men with a positive reduction in anxiety (Townsend, 1995). All this evidence reinforces the groundbreaking research conducted by Kinsey *et al.* (1948) into sexual behaviour in the 1940s, which concluded, 'There seems to be no question but that the human male would be promiscuous in his choice of sexual partners throughout the whole of his life if there were no social restrictions' and that 'the human female is much less interested in a variety of partners'.

However, there is an obvious problem with the idea that men are having frequent casual sex whereas women are not. Who are these men having their encounters with? Can it really be that there are a few women having casual sex with thousands of men? Or are men exaggerating the number of sexual encounters in equal proportion to women who are under-reporting theirs? Much of the research is based on *reported* rather than *actual* behaviour and different attitudes to the reporting process may influence how people respond. As the comedians suggest, there may be greater stigma associated with female promiscuity – and this could well have affected some of the research. It would be interesting to know whether women feel this stigma as strongly today, now that we have experienced the 'ladette' culture.

Over-reliance on reported information is not, of course, a problem when we are able simply to observe the behaviours for ourselves. The differing sexual behaviour of males and females was famously, if perhaps apocryphally, observed by the US president Calvin Coolidge (1872–1973) when visiting a chicken farm in Kentucky, where he and his wife were taken on separate conducted tours. When Mrs Coolidge asked why there was only one cockerel, she was told that the cockerel could copulate dozens of times each day. Suitably impressed, she responded, 'Please tell that to the President'. Initially, the President was dumbfounded. He then asked if the cockerel always copulated with the same hen. On being told, 'Oh no, Mr President, it's a different hen each time' he nodded wisely and said, 'Please tell that to Mrs Coolidge'. The finding that males can be kept aroused for long periods with the continued introduction of different females is now known as the 'Coolidge effect'. The Coolidge effect may also be noted in humans. When Wilson (1989) asked men and women if they were getting enough sex, 56 per cent of the men and 41 per cent of the women replied that they were not. Of greater note, however, is the fact that 37 per cent of the men and only 18 per cent of the women reported that they would like 'more partners'; 63 per cent of the women and only 38 per cent of the men said that they would like more sex with their regular partner.

Having acknowledged that there is a great deal of truth in this stereotype, let's consider why it is that men want more sex, and with more partners, than women. Throughout the animal kingdom, males generally appear to be more easily aroused than females: some male frogs will mate with anything that vaguely resembles a female; houseflies will try to seduce a knotted bootlace. The answer is that it makes evolutionary sense for a male to have multiple partners, each of whom can produce his offspring – whereas a female who has selected her mate gains nothing from the sperm of others. The male sower of wild oats increases his chances of reproductive success whereas the promiscuous woman risks disease, jealous violence and being left to raise her children alone. So the genes of promiscuous men prosper, whilst those of promiscuous women die out. Of course our desire to have sex is not necessarily a conscious expression of our desire to reproduce. Thanks to the brain's limbic system, which controls primitive drives and reminds us to send our genes into the future, we also have sex because we enjoy it. An orgasm gives us a 'high' on the chemical dopamine, which regulates feelings of pleasure, and the Coolidge effect ensures that this high may be achieved frequently. And that's good news for our sense of wellbeing as well as our genes.

To end on a note of caution: it would, of course, be misleading to suggest that *no* women engage in casual sex, just as it would be misleading to suggest that *all* men do. We also need to remember that the evolutionary reasons that account for this phenomenon do not make a valid excuse for male promiscuity ...

➡ *See also* The gold-digging woman and the looks-obsessed man; The porn-obsessed man; The sex-obsessed man.

The stressed-out grey-haired person

I t is popularly reported that the hair of both Thomas More and Marie Antoinette turned white in a matter of hours the night before their executions, as a reaction to the extreme stress of impending death. Although rarely seen to happen so quickly – and certainly not in such dramatic circumstances – there is a widely-held belief that stress causes grey hair. Because grey hair is associated with old age, and is therefore something that we are anxious to avoid for as long as possible, speculation on this subject is a source of endless fascination.

The greying process starts in the follicles, which are tiny cavities in the scalp. Typically, we have 100,000 of these cavities, each of which can grow several hairs in a lifetime. At the base of each follicle there are skin cells of two different types. Keratinocytes make keratin, a colourless protein that manufactures each hair and gives it its texture and strength. Melanocytes produce a pigment called melanin, which is delivered to the keratinocytes. Melanin comes in two shades that combine to create a vast array of human hair colours. Hair that has lost most of its melanin is grey, and eventually turns white (Ballantyne, 2007).

There are marked individual differences in the age at which the first few grey hairs appear, but this usually happens around the age of 30 for men and 35 for women. There is considerable debate as to whether stress hormones might impair the production of melanin or whether it is more a case of heredity – with some of us being predisposed to premature grey hair simply because it runs in the family. Hanjani and Cymet (2003) suggest that going grey is predominantly determined by our genes, but that stress and other lifestyle factors can make onset earlier. Their view is that stress doesn't directly cause melanocyte cells to die more quickly, but it might contribute to hair loss – and the more often hair falls out and regrows, the quicker the pigment cells break down.

If this is the case, we might expect to see strong correlations between stress-related illness and grey hair. Schnohr *et al.* (1998) examined 13,000 men and women participating in the Copenhagen City Heart Study to see if any relationship existed between grey hair and mortality rates. Whilst they found little direct correlation, they did observe that a small number of men who had no grey hair at all had a significantly lower mortality rate. A strong correlation exists between smoking and the early onset of grey hair for both men and women, although again no direct cause-and-effect relationship has been found (Mosley and Gibbs, 1996).

So what happened to Marie Antoinette? There is an extremely rare condition called telogen effluvium in which major stress speeds up hair loss of the kind described by Hanjani and Cymet – although this typically occurs between one and three months after the stressful incident. If Marie Antoinette or Thomas More had a mix of dark and grey hair, perhaps it was sudden hair loss that made their hair look whiter 'overnight'. In Marie Antoinette's case, however, it is far more likely that she simply stopped wearing her wig, revealing the natural grey hair that she had previously concealed.

If you have grey hair, don't get stressed out about it – although if you do it's unlikely to make matters worse. If you're a woman and your grey hair bothers you, you could always avail yourself of some of the many hair colouring products now available. If you're a man, take comfort from the fact that grey-haired George Clooney, the Oscar®-winning actor, is widely recognized as one of the sexiest men in the world.

➡ *See also* The dumb blonde; The gentleman who prefers blondes; The passionate redhead.

The stupid WAG

Whilst footballers are renowned for their skills on the pitch, their wives and girlfriends (sometimes referred to as WAGs) are famous for their expensive shopping trips. They are usually stereotyped as stupid airheads whose only interests are designer handbags and the acquisition of a fake tan (usually tinged with orange).

The 'matching hypothesis' suggests that two people are more likely to become romantically involved if they are closely matched in terms of their ability to 'reward' one another. In practice, we usually have to accept a compromise and settle for the best match that we can realistically hope to find – a partner who can bring to the relationship qualities that are roughly comparable to those that we can offer in return (Gross and Rolls, 2006).

Professional football in Britain is a low-brow occupation, albeit an extremely well-paid one. Despite the fact that over 40 per cent of the UK population now go to university, few footballers do so. Footballers are not considered the most articulate of people – listen to a post-match interview and you will understand why – and their WAGs are sometimes tarred with the same brush. It is assumed that these not-so-bright men tend to attract stupid women who match them in the intelligence stakes.

However, we must not underrate these ladies. Of the twelve WAGs of professional footballers who are most often mentioned in the newspapers, nine have five or more GCSE passes (grades A* to C); of these, one has ten GCSEs (including four 'A' grades), two have three good A level passes and another two have, or are in the midst of, university degrees. Add to this the fact that two had already forged successful careers in pop before falling for · their famous footballers and the picture improves further. Such are the achievements of this much maligned dozen that in 2007 the Learning and Skills Council, which aims to improve the skills of young people, used these individuals as role models in a campaign that aimed to encourage more teenage girls to stay on at school rather than dropping out at 16.

The negative stereotyping that the WAGs often attract must be a cause of some annoyance to them. Psychologists have noted that people have different methods for coping with being negatively stereotyped. Some ignore the criticism ('other people are just jealous'); some react and try to argue that the stereotyping is untrue. Others simply disassociate themselves from the target group, as did one of the current WAGS: 'It's like a comedy. Everyone's so flash ... Footballers' wives are just as bad as benefit scroungers, it's just a higher class of scrounger'.

The evidence suggests that the stereotyping of some WAGs as ignorant bimbos is most unfair. A relationship is like a game of football in that it requires two halves and each WAG makes a valuable contribution to her marriage or relationship. The current WAGs are far more educated than their partners – and given the 'matching hypothesis', this is more than we might expect. Yes, it's true that they enjoy shopping, but the mere fact that they use their partners' credit cards must dispel any remaining doubts as to their intelligence. If your partner is a multimillionaire you'd surely be stupid not to spend some of it.

The violent madman

Throughout history, people with mental illnesses have been feared, misunderstood and neglected. Only a few hundred years ago, some of those with mental health problems were thought to be witches and burnt at the stake; for many years 'lunatics' were confined to large asylums and even in the 20th century some mental health patients were restrained using straitjackets. Since time immemorial, people with mental illnesses have been treated as second-class citizens. This ignorant attitude has often led to their being lumbered with stigmatizing labels, and one phrase that has come into common usage in recent years is 'mad, bad and dangerous to know'. These words are attributed to Lady Caroline Lamb, who used them to describe her controversial lover, the Romantic poet Lord Byron (1788–1824); today, the phrase is commonly used with reference to the mentally ill. Is there research evidence suggesting that the mentally ill are more likely to be 'dangerous' or 'bad' – and could they ever be described as 'mad'?

Let's start with the allegation that the mentally ill might be violent, threatening the safety of the individual. Our chances of being confronted by an 'axe-wielding maniac' are thankfully remote. However, several high-profile cases – for example, the murder in 1996 of Lin and Megan Russell by Michael Stone, who had suffered from severe mental disturbance – have caused the media to suggest a link between mental ill health and violence. It is true that there is a clear relationship between the two: contrary to expectations, the mentally ill are four times more likely than others to be the *victims* of a verbal or physical attack. It is rare that people with mental health difficulties are the perpetrators of violence. During 2002/03, less than five per cent of the 873 homicides that took place in England and Wales were attributed to people with suspected mental health problems (Povey, 2004). A study by Taylor and Gunn (1999) about care in the community and perceived 'dangerousness' of the mentally ill concluded: 'There is no evidence that it is anything but stigmatizing to claim that their living in the community is a dangerous experience that should be reversed'.

Could a person with mental health problems be in any way 'bad'? For thousands of years people believed that the bizarre behaviour associated with mental illness was the result of possession by evil spirits and demons. In some cultures these unfortunates were tortured in a futile attempt at exorcism. Nowadays, thankfully, no one in their right mind believes that the mentally ill are to blame for their mental health problems. Having appendicitis doesn't make you 'bad', so why should any other type of medical condition?

The one remaining label – 'mad' – is not a diagnostic term that would be used by a mental health professional today; it is a generic term meaning 'suffering from a disorder of the mind'. Nevertheless, the term 'mad' is often used by lay people with regard to mental health problems. Some academics have questioned whether mental illness exists at all. Thomas Szasz, co-founder of the Citizens Commission on Human Rights, suggested that illness is a physical concept that cannot be applied to a psychological disorder. Taking this reasoning to its logical conclusion, he claimed that mental illness is a myth (Szasz, 1972). Although this idea – and the so-called 'anti-psychiatry' movement – gained a lot of support in the 1970s, it is no longer taken seriously (Tantum, 1991).

I'd now like to turn my attention to labelling in general as applied to people with mental health problems. First I must stress my belief that mental illness does, of course, exist – and has long-term damaging effects. However, 'labelling theory' suggests that mental disorders are sometimes 'created' for people who do not conform to the social norms. Since these norms are subjective and vary across cultures, the diagnosis of mental illness is fraught with problems. Once labelled as mentally ill a patient's condition often worsens and the label can, it seems, become a self-fulfilling prophecy. Worse still, the negative attitudes of others exacerbate and maintain the disorder.

Psychologist David Rosenhan, who was working at about the same time as Thomas Szasz, and influenced by some of the same ideas, set out to examine whether the diagnostic labels meted out by psychiatrists were accurate (Rosenhan, 1973). Could they reliably distinguish between the sane and the insane? In a brilliant study that demonstrates clearly how difficult it is to diagnose mental illness, Rosenhan arranged for eight individuals of sound mind to try to gain admission to mental hospitals by stating that they had been hearing voices saying the words 'empty' or 'thud'; on admission, they were to behave entirely normally. All eight pseudopatients were admitted to different hospitals and treated as though they had a mental disorder. Patronized and often ignored by hospital staff, the pseudopatients made notes on their experiences and even this behaviour was taken as a sign of mental illness ('compulsive note-taking'). Many of them found it difficult to relate to the other patients – and this too was viewed as a symptom. It was other patients, rather than the staff, who identified and challenged these 'fakes'. On average the pseudopatients were kept in hospital for 19 days, with one patient staying for 52. This study demonstrates that even psychiatrists can be influenced by the attachment of a label, which may blinker them from a true perception of a person's behaviour. If trained psychiatrists cannot distinguish the 'sane' from the 'insane', exactly who are we to call 'mad'?

Rosenhan then took his research a step further by informing another hospital that he would refer some pseudopatients over a three-month period; staff were asked to rate all new patients as 'genuine' or 'false'. Although Rosenhan sent no pseudopatients at all, doubts were raised over a significant number of the 193 patients admitted. Again we see that the boundaries between sanity and insanity are far from clear-cut. Echoes of this study can be seen in the 1975 Oscar®-winning film *One Flew Over the Cuckoo's Nest*, based on the novel of the same name by Ken Kesey and directed by Milos Forman. When the main protagonist, R P McMurphy (played by Jack Nicholson), is convicted for assault, his behaviour is thought to indicate mental illness; as a result, he is confined to a mental hospital.

The mentally ill do not conform to this or any other stereotype: labelling people in this way can have damaging consequences for all concerned. All of us, with or without mental health problems, are capable of acting 'mad', behaving 'bad' or being 'dangerous to know' at times and these behaviours are not the sole territory of the mentally ill. Yet the perceived connection between mental ill-health and violence remains deeply embedded in the public consciousness. How might this be overcome? Sensitive media coverage and educational initiatives might start to change our misconceptions. For example, stories about people who recover from mental illness or who continue to make important contributions to society whilst suffering from mental health problems (which would include the vast majority of such cases) would help to redress the balance. Let's hope that attitudes soon begin to change. Experiencing a mental health problem is difficult enough in itself without adding to this the burden of public prejudice.

➡ *See also* The dangerous stranger; The mad genius; The sadistic prison guard; The schizophrenic with the split personality.

The weaker sex

If it's physical strength we're talking about then there's no contest: men are physically stronger than women, who are undoubtedly the weaker of the two sexes. The winner of last year's World's Strongest Man competition was Mariusz Pudzianowski (nicknamed Super Mario). As he has won this competition five times in seven years he has a particularly good claim to the title. The four-times winner of the World Strongwoman Championships is Aneta Florczyk, though she doesn't come close to matching the 285kg bench press of Super Mario. Nevertheless, there is no doubt that Aneta is stronger than the majority of men.

The stereotype of women being the 'weaker sex' isn't just used in relation to physical prowess. Are women weaker than men in other areas of life as well? It seems not. There are 115 males conceived for every 100 females, but from that moment on males seem to be the weaker of the sexes. Male foetuses are less likely to survive to full term than females, although there are still slightly more boys born than girls (105 males for every 100 females). However, both neonatal death and sudden infant death syndrome are more common among boys than girls. The boys who do survive are more likely than girls are to suffer from autism or Tourette's syndrome or to experience dyslexia or learning disabilities (Jones, 2003).

One of boys' greatest weaknesses is in succumbing to peer pressure, which leads them into risk-taking behaviour; as a result, teenage boys are twice as likely as teenage girls to die in adolescence. However, the stereotype that it is boys, not girls, who hang around on street corners getting drunk is incorrect. In 2004, Martin Plant questioned 2,000 young people aged between 15 and 16 years about their drinking habits (Plant, 2004). For the first time ever in the UK, the total percentage of teenage girls who had indulged in binge drinking during the last month (consuming more than five units per session) was higher than that of boys (32 per cent compared to 25 per cent).

Having reached adulthood, men are more likely than women to be successful in taking their own lives, despite the fact that more women than men attempt suicide. By the age of 35 years, there are more women alive than men. Perhaps continuing their risk-taking behaviour as adults, men remain more vulnerable than women to accidents; they are also more likely to suffer from cancer, diabetes and heart disease. Despite these increased health risks, men visit the doctor 50 per cent less than women do, claiming that they don't have the time. Once they do see a doctor, embarrassment may prevent them from sharing their concerns. Perhaps these few facts alone explain why men may be more prone to some serious illnesses that would be treatable if diagnosed early. In the UK, men tend to die about five years earlier than women: life expectancy is currently 81 years for women and 76 years for men. By the age of 100 years, women outnumber men by approximately eight to one.

However there are some areas in which men appear to be stronger and more robust. Women tend to report more headaches than men and there are a few diseases and injuries that are more common among women. For example, women are more likely to suffer from osteoarthritis and rheumatoid arthritis and to be affected more severely by these conditions. Similarly, more women succumb to osteoporosis – and at a younger age than men

– and female athletes tend to experience more knee problems than their male counterparts. Some women blame men for the fact that depression is more common in women; however, the statistics may reflect a difference in reporting rates rather than a true variation in incidence.

It's commonly believed that women are the stronger sex when it comes to tolerating pain, perhaps because they cope so well with the pain of childbirth. However, research suggests that this may not be the case: women tend to report more pain, in more bodily areas, occurring more frequently and lasting longer. One way of measuring pain is using a cold pressor tank. Volunteers place one arm in a warm bath (37°C) for two minutes before transferring it to an ice-cold bath (maintained at 1°C or 2°C) for a maximum of two minutes. Researchers then take two measurements: the point at which volunteers first notice the pain (the pain threshold) and the point at which they can no longer stand it (the pain tolerance level). Results show that men have a higher pain threshold, as well as a higher pain tolerance level. This difference in pain perception may be due to a combination of hormonal, social and cultural factors. Alternatively, it may be that the two sexes experience pain in a qualitatively differently way: research suggests that women focus on emotional aspects whereas men concentrate more on the physical sensations (Keogh, 2008; Mitchell *et al.*, 2004).

So much for the differences between the sexes in their ability to survive physically. What about our abilities to succeed in life? Since the late 1960s, boys' levels of educational achievement have fallen behind those of girls. According to the Joseph Rowntree Foundation, boys outnumber girls as low achievers in UK schools by a ratio of three to two (Cassen and Kingdon, 2007). These figures are now reflected in occupational settings, where women are beginning to take a larger percentage of jobs in professions that have traditionally been dominated by men. In 2005, 63 per cent of accountancy apprenticeships were taken by women; 62 per cent of law students and 58 per cent of medicine and dentistry graduates were women (*The Observer*, 2007).

On balance, it looks rather as though men may be the weaker sex. Sykes (2003) claims that male infertility is increasing as sperm counts decline – perhaps because of pesticides – and that men will die out completely within the next 5,000 generations. Within the next 125,000 years, Sykes predicts, the human race will rely on female unisex reproduction in the laboratory. What can we do to prevent this? Perhaps the inaccurate perception of women as the weaker sex has led to our paying too little attention to men's health issues over the years. This needs to be rectified as soon as possible before men disappear altogether – leaving women not just the stronger but the only remaining sex.

➡ *See also* The emotional woman; The headache-prone woman.

The wicked stepmother

The noun 'stepmother' is nearly always preceded by the adjective 'wicked'. In 'Snow White and the Seven Dwarfs', the wicked stepmother (seen here) is horrified when the magic mirror tells her that her stepdaughter Snow White is more beautiful than she is – and as a result she bribes someone to murder the girl. In both 'Hansel and Gretel' and 'Cinderella' the stepmother characters are portrayed as equally cruel, unfair and unloving (Dainton, 1993). Mothers and their daughters, on the other hand, are beautiful, kind and loving. End of (fairy) story? No, not quite.

Bettelheim (1989) proposed that the wicked stepmother in fairy tales may serve a useful purpose, acting as an emotional buffer for the audience – particularly for the children at whom most of these stories are aimed. Whereas the idea of a cruel tormentor cast as a mother might be too intense, placing her in the role of stepmother puts her at one remove from the child, allowing him or her to give full rein to any feelings of anger or fear without guilt. In many instances, this may allow children to deal with negative thoughts or images concerning their real mother. Since mothers are widely assumed to be full to the brim with love and goodness, any negative feelings towards them are best displaced, disguised, or redirected at stepmothers instead (Watson, 1995).

Now let's consider a few facts about stepfamilies in general. The word 'step' comes from an Old English word meaning 'related by marriage rather than blood'. This word is also associated with bereavement or loss, and in reference to stepmothers it might carry with it several different connotations – such as, 'one step removed', 'second best', or 'stepping into someone else's shoes'. The ancient Greeks and Romans thought that the negative attitude shown by a stepmother towards her stepchildren was a normal feature of the relationship. This was reflected in various phrases of the time: for example, a good day would be described as a 'mother day' and a bad day as a 'stepmother day' (Roesch, 2007).

Stepfamilies happen when one parent loses a spouse through death or divorce, and then remarries. Given that many marriages now fail, there are growing numbers of step-parents. Stepfamilies are growing faster than any other family type, with approximately two and a half million children growing up within stepfamilies in the UK in 2004 (Doodson and Morley, 2006). In 1993, Misrach estimated that one in three Americans belonged to a stepfamily (Misrach, 1993). Since many children stay with their mother following a divorce, there are far more stepfathers than stepmothers living in stepfamilies. A small number of step-parents most certainly do deserve the 'wicked' epithet. Daly and Wilson (1996) investigated whether parents were more likely to neglect, assault, exploit or otherwise mistreat their stepchildren than their genetic children. They found that, in the USA, stepchildren constituted a much higher proportion of child abuse victims than did those children who remained in their birth families. Subsequent research confirmed this as a universal finding across a number of different cultures.

The youngest children rarely have step-parents; when they do, however, studies in Canada, Britain and the United States indicate that their risk of being murdered by a step-parent is between 50 and 100 times higher than their risk of being murdered by a biological parent. Having a step-parent has turned out to be the single most powerful predictor of severe child maltreatment yet discovered. Of course, there are many other factors that might explain these findings: for example, poverty, unemployment or a history of abuse in the family. The researchers found that the great majority of abuse and homicide cases among step-parents were perpetrated by men, which makes you wonder why stepfathers don't get a bad press too. However, they had no clear evidence that stepmothers constitute a lesser threat – they simply found that the numbers of stepmothers living with stepchildren were too small for the figures to be reliable.

One study examined the (step)mother–(step)child relationship among college students in three family types: those with a stepmother or a stepfather, and intact biological families. Young people in stepmother families generally saw themselves as being in a poorer quality of relationship, lacking support and more often in conflict with their stepmother. However, when the views of these students were compared to those living with their biological mothers in other family types, it became apparent that they were not conscious of more overall family conflict or less family cohesion than others. So young people may report more conflict with a stepmother but not more family conflict in general (Pruett *et al.*, 1993).

Stepmothers are an easy scapegoat for conflict in stepfamilies. It doesn't help that there are aspects of any stepfamily situation that cause tensions which may reinforce the stereotype. When children do not appear to prosper in a second marriage it is often found that their problems started long before the second marriage took place and was as a result of parental conflict prior to the divorce. However, given the strong and enduring stereotype of stepmothers it is often easier to blame any disquiet on a new stepmother than on one's biological parents (Furstenberg and Cherlin, 2006) – in fact, stepmothers often blame themselves for their adopted children's unhappiness. If the biological mother feels some hostility to her husband's new wife, the children may feel and understand her resentment. The children also see that their father loves his new wife; they may find it difficult to reconcile these opposing forces and, unsurprisingly, the result can sometimes be emotional turmoil. Moreover, because a remarried father often feels guilt about the failure of his first marriage, he may overindulge the children. The stepmother, who typically spends more time at home with the children, is left to discipline them and may therefore be regarded as cruel – whereas a biological mother acting in exactly the same way might be praised for setting clear boundaries for her children's behaviour.

There are further plausible reasons that explain the origins of the wicked stepmother stereotype. It is likely that some stepmothers, despite putting a great deal of effort and love into the relationship with their stepchildren, may not engage with them quite as deeply as they would with their own biological children. It is usually the case that adults with dependent children are seen as less desirable in the marriage market than those without children. Many women who take on the role of stepmother may be less likely to have children of their own from the union; if they feel that they have missed out because of this, they may feel resentment towards their stepchildren. In other instances the stepmother may be jealous of the relationship her husband had with his former wife and this negative attitude may be focused on the children, who are a visible and constant reminder of it. Even if the stepmother experiences no such jealous feelings, she may simply resent having another woman's child living in her home.

However, the outlook is not all gloom for women who take on children in a new marriage. Being a stepmother can be a difficult job, but the vast majority do it successfully and can feel a real sense of accomplishment in bringing up their husband's offspring. The children can also benefit: from feeling loved by both their biological parents and from observing remarried adults in a successful loving relationship. Rutter, following a study using questionnaires and interviews, comments that 80 per cent of children cared for by a stepmother develop into fine adults with no behavioural problems whatsoever (Rutter, 1994).

Some researchers have suggested giving the old fairy tales new twists that show stepmothers in a better light. Call me old-fashioned but I think we should stick to the originals. I'm not sure that Cinderella's stepmother was so bad after all. She knew that Cinderella could not be trusted and therefore warned her not to stay out after midnight. The girl fell in love with the first bloke she danced with and stayed out contrary to instructions, making no plans for how to get home. Hardly ideal, was it? So was the stepmother really so wicked? Oh no she wasn't! I reckon she just knew what kind of a girl Cinderella really was ...

The woman who can't park and the man who can't pack

A car commercial on TV shows a woman being told by a couple of builders that she'll never get into the small parking space in front of their van. She promptly reverses up and over their van, using their scaffolding planks, and parks perfectly. This ad challenges the stereotype of women not being able to park – at the same time perpetuating the stereotype of the tea-drinking sexist builder. Not bad for one advert. But is the stereotype that women are bad drivers based on fact?

According to Pease and Pease (2001), some women are unable to park parallel to the kerb because their brains lack the clearly defined visual–spatial area that is needed for this kind of activity. It seems that there may be an evolutionary reason for this. Over many thousands of years, men have evolved neural circuits that equip them with all the skills that they need for hunting. Those men with well-developed spatial abilities are those who have survived long enough to pass on their genes to the next generation. Brain scans have shown that between 80 and 85 per cent of women have neural circuits that lack the spatial abilities that are almost universal in men. Researchers believe that this may explain women's difficulty with any activities that involve the estimation of space, distance and speed. Whilst men are good at map reading, women have gone on to develop those skills that are necessary in childcare – including the ability to communicate.

The views of Pease and Pease are controversial – perhaps deliberately so, since controversy has undoubtedly increased the sales of their book. They are frequently accused of sexism, and many people question the 'biology is destiny' argument. However, the researchers argue that it is not a case of one sex being better than the other; it is more a case of evolution equipping men and women with different skills. This is certainly one way of explaining behavioural differences between the sexes. A study that tentatively lends some support to the hypothesis of Pease and Pease was conducted by Deborah Saucier of the University of Saskatchewan in Canada (Telegraph.co.uk, 2002). She set up an experiment designed to compare the navigation skills of men and women. Participants were given tasks in map reading and in following a set of descriptive instructions; while the men performed best on the map-reading task, women did far better using the descriptive directions – which drew upon their communication skills.

So what about the stereotype that men can't pack? If we accept that this is primarily a visuo-spatial task then we would expect men to be better than women at doing this. However, the stereotype suggests that men are worse than women. Studies have consistently shown that, in general, women are excellent at seeing two-dimensions in the brain, but men are better at seeing a third dimension, namely depth. Again, this should mean that men are better at packing than women. However, success at such tasks does not merely reflect visuo-spatial ability but also depends on motivation and interest levels. Perhaps men are not as motivated as women to pack? Perhaps they are also less concerned with what they wear on holiday and therefore don't really care if they forget to pack their favourite shirt or enough clean undies for the week. I know of very few men who look forward to packing, and so maybe men have encouraged this 'can't pack' stereotype in order to avoid performing an onerous chore! I'm sure male sky-divers when asked to pack their own parachutes are probably sufficiently motivated to do a half decent job.

But the stereotype of women behind the wheel suggests not only that they can't park, but also that they are generally bad drivers. What is the origin of this? It is certainly not derived from accident statistics, since almost all of these show women to be safer drivers than men. Young female drivers have far fewer accidents then young male drivers – and this is reflected in their car insurance premiums. Although this gender difference is greatest among people below the age of 25 years, it is also evident among older drivers; the difference between the sexes in terms of fatalities on the road is marked for all age groups (Maycock *et al.*, 1991).

The St Louis Historical Society (2008) suggests that the first woman driver was Genevra Mudge of New York City, who took to the road in 1899 – and other women soon followed. At first, driving was limited to the affluent; these female drivers did not pose a threat to the established order and at this stage there was no negative stereotyping of women drivers. After World War I, however, women started to become more independent and it is suggested that their new-found status and confidence began to disturb, or some might say disrupt, the accepted social order. Negative stereotyping of women drivers soon became commonplace; feminists suggest that this was instigated by men as a way of keeping women in their place (Berger, 1986). Perhaps men perpetuate this stereotype even today: after all, when a couple go out together it is often the case that the man drives, with the woman as passenger. Of course, if he wants a drink then he's happy to let her drive home.

Statistics for the UK show that, in 2002, 88 per cent of all driving offences and 83 per cent of speeding offences were committed by men. If you ask a man to define the characteristics of a good driver, he may well answer in terms of how 'highly skilled' the driver is: so by his definition, a racing driver would be a good driver. When women are asked the same question, they answer in terms of how 'safe' the driver is and how competently he or she can get from A to B. This difference between the sexes is demonstrated in car driver research. Reason *et al.* (1990) developed a driver behaviour questionnaire to measure how often drivers make mistakes whilst driving. They classified these mistakes into three broad categories:

- **lapses** are mistakes that may be embarrassing but are not usually life-threatening (for example, trying to pull away from traffic lights in the wrong gear or hitting something when reversing);
- **errors** are potentially more serious and are typically misjudgements and failures of observation that may be hazardous to others (for example, failure to check mirrors when overtaking or failure to see a 'Stop' sign);
- **violations** are deliberate deviations from the practices that are deemed necessary for road safety (for example, deliberate disregard of speed limits, overtaking on the inside, racing, tailgating, drink-driving, and so on).

Statistically speaking, drivers who commit deliberate violations are more likely to have accidents than those who experience lapses or make errors on the road. Women and older drivers are more likely than other drivers to report lapses. However, male drivers – and particularly young male drivers – are more likely to commit violations. Why do they deliberately choose to take these risks? Perhaps because they believe they are better drivers than average; women, on the other hand, take a more realistic view of their own abilities. Believing yourself to be a better driver than average may arise from an unrealistic optimism bias; it can result in taking risks that are way beyond your capabilities.

In conclusion, women may be worse at parking than men and they may have a few more scratches on their bumpers as a result. However, these superficial blemishes are probably preferable to one massive dent in the roof – which reminds a man of the time when he deliberately drove too fast and found himself overturned in a ditch. Is a good driver a skilful driver or one who gets from A to B safely? Your answer may well reveal not only the way you drive but also your gender. Forget the racing drivers: a good driver is a safe driver. Women may not be able to parallel park or read maps quite as effectively as men, but they're certainly safer drivers.

And with regard to packing, I suggest any women reading this should encourage the men in their life to pack their own bags – the psychology suggests they should be good at it. In fact, perhaps men should offer to pack the bags for women as well as their own – they might find they have a lot less to carry.

References

References

Opening quotation
Burtt, E A (Ed), *The English Philosophers from Bacon to Mill*, Random House, New York, 1977

Introduction
Gilmartin, B, *Shyness and Love: Causes, Consequences and Treatment*, University Press of America, Maryland, 1987

Lee, Y-T, Jussim, L, and McCauley, C, *Stereotype Accuracy: Toward Appreciating Group Differences*, American Psychological Association, Washington DC, 1995

Sherif, M, Harvey, O J, White, B J, *et al.*, *Intergroup Cooperation and Conflict: The Robber's Cave Experiment*, University of Oklahoma Press, Norman, 1961

Steele, C M, and Aronson, J, 'Stereotype threat and the intellectual test performance of African Americans', *Journal of Personality and Social Psychology*, 69(5), 797–811, 1995

Walton, G M, and Cohen, G L, 'Stereotype lift', *Journal of Experimental Social Psychology*, 39(5), 456–67, 2003

Zimbardo, P, 'The Lucifer effect: how good people turn evil', lecture to psychology students and lecturers: the Emmanuel Centre, London, 18 March 2008

The aggressive shorty
Data on the height of US presidential candidates, winners and runners up available from www.swivel.com/data_columns/spreadsheet/4714193, accessed 5 January 2009

Case, A, and Paxson, C, *Stature and Status: Height, Ability and Labor Market Outcomes*, Working Paper 12466, National Bureau of Economic Research (NBER), Cambridge, Massachusetts, 2006, website: www.nber.org/papers/w12466, accessed 7 February 2008

Eslea, M, and Ritter, D, 'Short man syndrome – it's the bigger ones we have to look out for', *Catalyst Extra*, 1, 2007, Faculty of Science and Technology, University of Central Lancashire (UCLan), Preston, website: www.uclan.ac.uk/facs/science/Local/Catalyst.pdf, accessed 7 February 2008

Fleming, I, *Goldfinger*, Jonathan Cape, London, 1959 (current edn published by Penguin, Harmondsworth, 2002)

Heineck, G, 'Up in the skies? The relationship between body height and earnings in Germany', 2004, website: www.diw.de/documents/dokumentenarchiv/17/41848/paper2004_heineck.pdf, accessed 2 April 2008

Nettle, D, *Women's Height, Reproductive Success and the Evolution of Sexual Dimorphism in Modern Humans*, Departments of Biological Sciences and Psychology, The Open University, Milton Keynes, 2002

Persico, N, Postlewaite, A, and Silverman, D, *The Effect of Adolescent Experience on Labor Market Outcomes: The Case of Height*, Penn Institute for Economic Research (PIER) Working Paper 03–036, University of Pennsylvania, USA, 2003

The aphrodisiac oyster

Machen, A (translator), *Memoirs of Jacques Casanova de Seingalt, 1725–1798*, 1894, website: http://ebooks.adelaide.edu.au/c/casanova/c33m/c33m.html, accessed 26 May 2008

Mirza, R A, Poisson, J J, Fisher, G H, *et al.*, 'Do marine mollusks possess aphrodisiacal properties?', paper presented at the American Chemical Society Annual Meeting, San Diego, 16 March 2005

Shmerling, R, 2005, in: 'Oysters an aphrodisiac after all?', *Health News 24*, website: www.health24.com/news/Sexuality/1-944,31226.asp, accessed 14 April 2008

The big-footed man with the satisfied smile

Edwards, R, *The Definitive Penis Size Survey Results*, 6th edn, 2002, website: www.sizesurvey.com, accessed 22 January 2008

McCary, J L, *Sexual Myths and Fallacies*, Van Nostrand Reinhold Co., New York, 1–36, 1971

Shah, J, and Christopher, N, 'Can shoe size predict penile length?', *British Journal of Urology International*, 90, 586–7, 2002

Siminoski, K, and Bain, J, 'The relationships among height, penile length, and foot size', *Annals of Sex Research*, 6/3, 231–5, 1993

Wessels, H, Lue, T F, and McAninch, J W, 'Penile length in the flaccid and erect states: guidelines for penile augmentation', *Journal of Urology*, 156/3, 995–7, 1996

The boorish White Van Man

Automobile Association, 'White van men worth over £35 billion', 2007, website: www.theaa.com/motoring_advice/news/white-van-man.html, accessed 1 April 2008

Social Issues Research Centre (SIRC), *Renault Master White Van Man Study*, SIRC, Oxford, 1998, website: www.sirc.org/publik/white_van_man.html, accessed 7 December 2007

Social Issues Research Centre (SIRC), *The Renault 'New' Van Man Report: The Evolution of Silver Van Man*, SIRC, Oxford, 2003, website: www.sirc.org/wvm2003/index.shtml, accessed 6 December 2007

Walker, I, *Overtaking Bicycles in the UK: Cars versus White Light Goods Vehicles*, Department of Psychology, University of Bath, 2006, website: http://philica.com/index.php?discipline=24, accessed 5 December 2007

The boy in blue and the girl in pink

Hurlbert, A, and Ling, Y, 'Biological components of sex differences in colour preference', *Current Biology*, 17/16, 623–5, 2007

Isaacs, L D, 'Effects of ball size, ball color, and preferred color on catching by young children', *Perceptual and Motor Skills*, 51, 583–6, 1980

Ladies' Home Journal, June, 1918, viewed on website *Historical Boys' Clothing*, 1918: http://histclo.com/gender/col/col-pink.html, accessed 6 January 2008

Oram, N, Laing, D G, Hutchinson, I, *et al.*, 'The influence of flavor and color on drink identification by children and adults', *Developmental Psychobiology*, 28, 239–46, 1995

Picariello, M L, Greenberg, D N, and Pillemer, D B, 'Children's sex-related stereotyping of colors', *Child Development*, 61, 1453–60, 1990

Shoots, E, 'The effects of stereotypes and situational factors on children's favorite and preferred colors', Missouri Western State College, 5 December 1996, website: www.missouriwestern.edu/psychology/research/psy302/fall96/erin_shoots.html, accessed 6 January 2008

Smith, C, and Lloyd, B, 'Maternal behavior and perceived sex of infant: revisited', *Child Development*, 49/4, 1263–5, 1978

Will, J R, Self, P A, and Datan, N, 'Maternal behavior and perceived sex of infant', *American Journal of Orthopsychiatry*, 46, 135–9, 1976

The brainy first-born

Ansbacher, H L, and Ansbacher, R R (Eds), *The Individual Psychology of Alfred Adler*, Harper Torchbooks, New York, 1956

Ernst, C, and Angst, J, *Birth Order: Its Influence on Personality*, Springer-Verlag, Berlin and New York, 1983

Galton, F, *English Men of Science*, Macmillan, London, 1874

Harris, J R, *The Nurture Assumption: Why Children Turn Out the Way They Do*, Free Press, New York, 1998

Kristensen, P, and Bjerkedal, T, 'Explaining the relation between birth order and intelligence', *Science*, 316/5832, 1717, 22 June 2007

Sulloway, F, *Born to Rebel*, Pantheon, New York, 1996

The common names of common people

Birmingham, L, 'Stereotypical attitudes towards Christian names and gender may influence diagnosis', Annual meeting of the Royal College of Psychiatrists, Edinburgh, 2000

Busse, T, and Seraydarian, L, 'First names and popularity in grade school children', *Psychology in the Schools*, 16/1, 149–53, 1978

Deluzain, H E, 'Names and behaviour', 1996, website: www.behindthename.com/articles/1.php, accessed 29 January 2008

Garwood, G, 'First-name stereotypes as a factor in self-concept and school achievement', *Journal of Educational Psychology*, 68, 482–7, 1976

Gross, R D, *Psychology: The Science of Mind and Behaviour*, 5th edn, Hodder and Stoughton, London, 2005

Harari, H, and McDavid, J W, 'Name stereotypes and teachers' expectations', *Journal of Educational Psychology*, 65, 222–5, 1973

Jahoda, G, 'A note on Ashanti names and their relationship to personality', *British Journal of Psychology*, 45, 192–5, 1954

Leirer, V O, Hamilton, D, and Carpenter, S, 'Common first names as cues for inferences about personality', *Personality and Social Psychology Bulletin*, 8/4, 712–18, 1982

Pelham, B W, Mirenberg, M C, and Jones, J K, 'Why Susie sells seashells by the seashore: implicit egotism and major life decisions', *Journal of Personality and Social Psychology*, 82, 469–87, 2002

Steele, K M, and Smithwick, L E, 'First names and first impressions: a fragile relationship', *Sex Roles*, 21/7–8, 517–23, 1989

West, S, and Shults, T, 'Liking for common and uncommon first names', *Personality and Social Psychology Bulletin*, 2/3, 299–302, 1976

The creative left-hander

Batheja, M, and McManus, I C, 'Handedness in the mentally handicapped', *Developmental Medicine and Child Neurology*, 27, 63–8, 1985

Bragdon, A, and Gamon, D, *Brains that Work a Little Bit Differently*, Brainwave Books, 2004

Coren, S, *The Left-Hander Syndrome: The Causes and Consequences of Left-Handedness*, The Free Press/Macmillan, New York, 1992

Francks, C, Maegawa, S, Laurén, J, *et al.* (2007), 'LRRTM1 on chromosome 2p12 is a maternally suppressed gene that is associated paternally with handedness and schizophrenia', *Molecular Psychiatry*, 7 August 2007

Hardyck, C, and Petrinovich, L F, 'Left-handedness', *Psychological Bulletin*, 84, 385–404, 1977

Hepper, P, McCartney, G, and Shannon, E, 'Lateralised behaviour in first trimester human foetuses', *Neuropsychologia*, 36/6, 531–4, 1998

Lalumière, M L, Blanchard, R, and Zucker, K L, 'Sexual orientation and handedness in men and women: a meta-analysis', *Psychological Bulletin*, 126, 575–92, 2000

McManus, C, *Right Hand, Left Hand*, Weidenfeld and Nicolson, London, 2002

Raymond, M, Pontier, D, Dufour, A, *et al.*, 'Frequency-dependent maintenance of left-handedness in humans', *Proceedings of the Royal Society of London*, B, 263, 1627–33, 1996

Salvesen, K A, Vatten, L J, Eik-Nes, S H, *et al.*, 'Routine ultrasonography in utero and subsequent handedness and neurological development', *British Medical Journal*, 307, 159–64, 1993

Steele, J, and Mays, S, 'New findings on the frequency of left- and right-handedness in mediaeval Britain', 1995, website: www.ksc.kwansei.ac.jp/~jed/CompCult/brit-handed.html, accessed 28 February 2008

Waldfogel, J, 'Sinister and rich: the evidence that lefties earn more', 2006, website: www.slate.com/id/2147842, accessed 28 February 2008

Witelson, S F, and Pallie, W, 'Left hemisphere specialization for language in the newborn: neuroanatomical evidence of asymmetry', *Brain*, 88, 653–62, 1973

The dangerous stranger

Barker, M, 'Women, children and the construction of evil', 2008, website: www.wickedness.net/Barker.pdf, accessed 4 February 2008

Baumeister, R F, *Evil: Inside Human Violence and Cruelty*, W H Freeman and Co., New York, 1996

Bureau of Justice Statistics, *Sex Offenses and Offenders: An Analysis of Data on Rape and Sexual Assault*, National Criminal Justice (NCJ) 163392, US Department of Justice, Washington DC, 1997

Cawson, P, Wattam, C, Brooker, S, *et al.*, *Child Maltreatment in the United Kingdom: A Study of the Prevalence of Child Abuse and Neglect*, National Society for the Prevention of Cruelty to Children (NSPCC), London, 2000

Koss, M P, Gidycz, C A, and Wisniewski, N, 'The scope of rape: incidence and prevalence of sexual aggression and victimisation in a national sample of higher education students', *Journal of Consulting and Clinical Psychology*, 55, 162–70, 1987

Lees, S, *Carnal Knowledge: Rape on Trial*, Penguin, Harmondsworth, 1996

Madriz, E, *Nothing Bad Happens to Good Girls: Fear of Crime in Women's Lives*, University of California Press, Berkeley, 1997

Soothill, K, and Walby, S, *Sex Crime in the News*, Routledge, London, 1991

The dirty old man

Waynforth, D, and Dunbar, R I M, 'Conditional mate choice strategies in humans: evidence from "lonely hearts" advertisements', *Behaviour*, 132, 755–79, 1995

The dowdy librarian

Carmichael, J V, 'The male librarian and the feminine image: a survey of stereotype, status, and gender perceptions', *Library and Information Science Research*, 14/4, 411–46, 1992

Green, P, 'Librarian survey: the warrior librarian', 2005, website: http://warriorlibrarian.com/RESEARCH/stereotype.html, accessed 8 March 2008

Kirkendall, C A, 'Of Princess Di, Richard Dawson, and the *Book Review Digest*: how bibliographic instruction librarians are changing stereotypes of librarians', *Research Strategies*, 4, 40–2, 1986

Morrizey, L, and Case, D, 'There goes my image: the perception of male librarians by colleague, student, and self', *College and Research Libraries*, 49/5, 453–64, 1988

Paul, M, and Evans, J, 'The librarians' self-starter: 100s of questions to challenge your thinking about your image, the profession's image, your job and your future', Freelance Library and Information Services of Australia, Camberwell, Victoria, 1988

Stelmakh, V, *The Image of the Library: Studies and Views from Several Countries: Collection of Papers*, University of Haifa Library, Haifa, 1994

Walker, S, and Lawson, L, 'The librarian stereotype and the movies', *Media and Culture (MC) Journal: The Journal of Academic Media Librarianship*, 1/1, 16–28, 1993

The dumb blonde

Bargh, J A, Chen, M, and Burrows, L, 'Automaticity of social behavior: direct effects of trait construct and stereotype activation on action', *Journal of Personality and Social Psychology*, 71, 230–44, 1996

Bry, C, Follenfant, A, and Meyer, T, 'Blonde like me: when self-construals moderate stereotype priming effects on intellectual performance', *Journal of Experimental Social Psychology*, in press, website: http://clem.bry.free.fr/, accessed 8 January 2008

Cassidy, T and Harris, G, 'The colour of your hair may leave you open to stereotypes and prejudice', paper presented at the British Psychological Society Annual Conference, Belfast, 1999

Dijksterhuis, A, and van Knippenberg, A, 'The relation between perception and behavior, or how to win a game of Trivial Pursuit', *Journal of Experimental Social Psychology*, 74, 865–77, 1998

Frank, R, 'Despite the dumb jokes, stereotypes may reflect some smart choices', *New York Times*, 7 June 2007

Kanazawa, S, and Kovar, J, 'Why beautiful people are more intelligent', *Intelligence*, 32, 227–43, 2004

Loos, A, *Gentlemen Prefer Blondes: The Illuminating Diary of a Professional Lady*, Boni Liveright, New York, 1925

Pitman, J, *On Blondes*, Bloomsbury, New York, 2003

The emotional woman

BPS, 'Can men get PMS?', *Conference Report*, 2004, website: www.bps.org.uk/ media–centre/press–releases/releases$/division–of–health–psychology/ can–men–get–pms.cfm, accessed 25 March 2008

Canli, T, Desmond, J E, Zhao, Z, *et al.*, 'Sex differences in the neural basis of emotional memories', *Proceedings of the National Academy of Sciences of the United States of America*, 99, 10789–94, Washington DC, 2002

Caplan, P, *They Say You're Crazy*, Perseus Books, New York, 1995

Fujita, F, Diener, E, and Sandvik, E, 'Gender differences in negative affect and well-being: the case for emotional intensity', *Journal of Personality and Social Psychology*, 61, 427–34, 1991

Levant, R, 'Men and emotions: a psychoeducational approach', *Assessment and Treatment of Psychological Disorders* Video Series, Newbridge Communications Inc., New York, 1997

Owen, P, 'Premenstrual syndrome', 2005, website: www.netdoctor.co.uk/ diseases/facts/pms.htm, accessed 22 May 2008

Witchalls, C, 'Boys don't cry', *Guardian*, 5 February 2003, website: http:// lifeandhealth.guardian.co.uk/family/story/0,,1609109,00.html, accessed 22 May 2008

The faithful hound

Banks, M, 'Man's best friend', *Anthrozoo*, 18/4, 2006, website: www.sciencedaily. com/releases/2006/01/060108215831.htm, accessed 4 January 2008

Biello, D, 'Genetic secrets of man's best friend revealed', *Scientific American*, 8 December 2005

BizRate Research Survey, 1–3 March 2005, website: http://findarticles. com/p/ articles/mi_m0EIN/is_2005_March_30/ai_n13489499, accessed 4 January 2008

Chambers, *The Chambers Dictionary*, Chambers Harrap Publishers Ltd, Edinburgh, 2008

Congressional Record, 'Eulogy on the Dog,' speech during lawsuit, 1870', 16 October 1914, 51, Appendix, 1235–6, Washington DC, 1914

Laino, C, reviewed by Chang, L, '"Dog visits help heart failure patients" study: hospitalized people with heart failure improve after a visit from man's best friend', WebMD Medical News, 15 November 2005, website:

www.webmd.com/heart-disease/heart-failure/news/20051115/dog-visits-help-heart-failure-patients, accessed 9 April 2008

Morey, D, 'Burying key evidence: the social bond between dogs and people', *Journal of Archaeological Science*, 33/2, 158–75, 2006

Newton, M, *Savage Girls and Wild Boys: A History of Feral Children*, Faber and Faber, London, 2002

Pavlov, I, *Conditioned Reflexes*, Oxford University Press, Oxford, 1927

Reagan, R, 'Man's best friend', website: www.msnbc.msn.com/id/7791682/, 13 May 2005, accessed 6 January 2008

Walton, B, '15,000 years with man's best friend', Cable News Network (CNN.com), website: http://edition.cnn.com/2002/TECH/science/11/21/coolsc.dogorigin/index.html, accessed 22 November 2002, and website: www.tolweb.org/treehouses/?treehouse_id=3804, accessed 8 January 2008

Wiseman, R, Smith, M, and Milton, J, 'Can animals detect when their owners are returning home? An experimental test of the "psychic pet" phenomenon', *British Journal of Psychology*, 89/3, 453–62, 1998

The football hooligan

Armstrong, G, 'False Leeds', in: Giulianotti, R, and Williams, J (Eds), *Game Without Frontiers*, Avebury, Aldershot, 1994

Armstrong, G, *Football Hooligans: Knowing the Score*, Berg Publishers, Oxford, 1998

Dunning, E G, Murphy, P, and Williams, J, *The Roots of Football Hooliganism*, Routledge, London, 1988

Finn, G P T, 'Football violence: a societal psychological perspective', in: Giulianotti, R, Bonney, N, and Hepworth, M (Eds), *Football Violence and Social Identity*, pp.90–127, Routledge, London, 1994

Le Bon, G, *The Crowd: A Study of the Popular Mind*, 1895, website: http://emotional-literacy-education.com/classic-books-online-b/tcrwd10.htm, accessed 15 November 2007

Marsh, P, Rosser, E, and Harré, R, *The Rules of Disorder*, Routledge, London, 1978

Stott, C, and Adang, O, 'Crowd psychology and public order policing', paper presented to the Policia de Segurança Pública (PSP) conference, Instituto Superior de Ciências Policiais e Segurança Interna, Lisbon, Portugal, 19

December 2003, notes on website: www.liv.ac.uk/Psychology/staff/CStott/
Accomp_Notes_Strategy_Conf_.pdf accessed 4 March 2008

Turner, R, and Killian, L, *Collective Behavior*, 2nd edn, Prentice Hall, Inc., New
Jersey, 1972 (3rd edn, 1987; 4th edn, 1993)

Williams, J, 'Who you calling a hooligan?' in: Perryman, M (Ed), *Hooligan
Wars*, Mainstream Publishing, Edinburgh, 2001

The funny clown

BBC News, 'Colombia clowns killed on stage', website: http://news.bbc.
co.uk/1/hi/world/americas/6382919.stm, 21 February 2007, accessed 5
May 2008

BBC News, 'Hospital clown images "too scary"', website: http://news.bbc.
co.uk/go/pr/fr/-/2/hi/health/7189401.stm, 15 January 2008, accessed 17
January 2008

Rohrer, F, 'Why are clowns scary?', BBC News, 16 January 2008, website:
http://news.bbc.co.uk/go/pr/fr/–/2/hi/health/7189401.stm   2008/01/15,
accessed 17 January 2008

Svebak, S, 'Health effects of sense of humor', paper presented at the
International Society for Humor Studies (ISHS) 18th Conference, Danish
University of Education, Copenhagen, Denmark, 2006, summary on
website: www.dpu.dk/site.aspx?p=8649andnewsid1=4306, accessed 17
January 2008

The gentleman who prefers blondes

Frost, P, 'European hair and eye color: a case of frequency-dependent sexual
selection?', *Evolution and Human Behavior*, 27/2, 85–103, 2006

Juni, S, and Michelle Roth, M, 'The influence of hair color on eliciting help: do
blondes have more fun?' *Social Behavior and Personality: An International
Journal*, 13/1, 11–14, 1985

Lawson, E D, 'Hair color, personality, and the observer', *Psychological Reports*,
28/1, 311–12, 1971

Loos, A, *Gentlemen Prefer Blondes: The Illuminating Diary of a Professional Lady*,
Boni Liveright, New York, 1925

Miller, A, and Kanazawa, S, *Why Beautiful People Have More Daughters: From
Dating, Shopping and Praying to Going to War and Becoming a Billionaire*

– *Two Evolutionary Psychologists Explain Why We Do What We Do*, Perigee Books, New York, 2007

Rich, M, and Cash, T, 'The American image of beauty: media representations of hair color for four decades', *Sex Roles*, 29/2, 113–24, 1993

Sorokowski, P, 'Do men prefer blonde women? The influence of hair colour on the perception of age and attractiveness of women', *Psychological Studies*, 44/3, 77–88, 2006

Thelen, T H, 'Minority type human mate preference', *Social Biology*, 30, 162–80, 1983

Unilever, '21st century man: wants brains, sophistication and equality', 2005, website: www.unilever.co.uk/ourcompany/newsandmedia/ pressreleases/2005/sunsilk16sept05.asp , accessed 5 January 2008

The gold-digging woman and the looks-obsessed man

BBC News, 'The lure of the older woman', website: http://news.bbc.co.uk/1/ hi/health/1410495.stm, 27 June 2001, accessed 13 March 2008

Betzig, L, *Despotism and Differential Reproduction: A Darwinian View of History*, Aldine de Gruyter, Hawthorne, New York, 1986

Betzig, L, 'Causes of conjugal dissolution: a cross-cultural study', *Current Anthropology*, 30, 654–76, 1989

Buss, D M, 'Sex differences in human mate preferences: evolutionary hypotheses tested in 37 cultures', *Behavioral and Brain Sciences*, 12, 1–49, 1989

Buss, D, and Malamuth, N (Eds), *Sex, Power, Conflict: Evolutionary and Feminist Perspectives*, Oxford University Press, New York, 1996

Cunningham, M R, 'Measuring the physical in physical attractiveness: quasi-experiments on the sociobiology of female facial beauty', *Journal of Personality and Social Psychology*, 50, 925–35, 1986

Dunbar, R, 'Are you lonesome tonight?', *New Scientist*, 11 April 1995

Singh, D, 'Adaptive significance of female physical attractiveness: role of waist–hip ratio', *Journal of Personality and Social Psychology*, 65, 293–307, 1993

Strassberg, D S, and Holty, S, 'An experimental study of women's internet personal ads', *Archives of Sexual Behavior*, 32, 253–60, 2003

Townsend, J M, and Levy, G D, 'Effects of potential partners' physical attractiveness and socioeconomic status on sexuality and partner selection: sex differences in reported preferences of university students', *Archives of Sexual Behavior*, 19, 149–64, 1990

Waynforth, D, and Dunbar, R I M, 'Conditional mate choice strategies in humans: evidence from "lonely hearts" advertisements', *Behaviour*, 132, 755–79, 1995

Zahavi, A, 'Mate selection: a selection for handicap', *Journal of Theoretical Biology*, 53, 205–14, 1975

The good Samaritan

Brooks, A C, 'Religious faith and charitable giving', *Policy Review*, 121, October/November 2003

Chambers, *Chambers Compact Dictionary*, Chambers Harrap Publishers Ltd, Edinburgh, 2005

Colasanto, D, 'Americans show commitment to helping those in need', *Gallup Report*, 284, 34–8, 1989

Curlin, F A, Dugdale, L S, Lantos, J D, *et al.*, 'Do religious physicians disproportionately care for the underserved?', *Annals of Family Medicine*, 5, 353–60, 2007

Darley, J M, and Batson, C D, 'From Jerusalem to Jericho: a study of situational and dispositional variables in helping behavior', *Journal of Personality and Social Psychology*, 27, 100–08, 1973

Dixon, D, and Abbey, S, 'Religious altruism and organ donation', *Psychosomatics*, 41, 407–11, 2000

Koenig, L, McGue, M, Krueger, R, *et al.*, 'Religiousness, antisocial behavior, and altruism: genetic and environmental mediation', *Journal of Personality*, 75/2, 265–90, 2007

Myers, D, *Social Psychology*, 8th edn, McGraw-Hill, New York, 2005

The gourmet Frenchman, the tight-fisted Scot and the serious German

BBC News, 'US people getting fatter, fast', website: http://news.bbc.co.uk/1/hi/health/4183086.stm, 2005, accessed 13 March 2008

Commission for Distilled Spirits, *World Drink Trends 2004*, World Advertising Research Center, Henley on Thames, 2004

Gilovich, T, *How We Know What Isn't So: The Fallibility of Human Reason in Everyday Life*, The Free Press, New York, 1993

Kunda, Z, 'The case for motivated reasoning', *Psychological Bulletin*, 108, 480–98, 1990

Madon, S, Guyll, M, Aboufadel, K, *et al.*, 'Ethnic and national stereotypes: the Princeton trilogy revisited and revised', *Personality and Social Psychological Bulletin*, 27/8, 996–1010, 2001

Nickerson, R, 'Confirmation bias: a ubiquitous phenomenon in many guises', *Review of General Psychology*, 2/2, 175–220, 1998

Terracciano, A and McCrae, R, 'National character does not reflect mean personality trait levels in 49 cultures', *Science*, 310/5745, 96–100, 2005

Wason, P, 'On the failure to eliminate hypotheses in a conceptual task', *Quarterly Journal of Experimental Psychology*, 12, 129–48, 1960

The grim North

Charter, D, 'It's grim down South and happy up North', website: www.timesonline.co.uk/tol/news/world/europe/article1662890.ece, 17 April 2007, accessed 14 February 2008

Day, E, 'North v South', *Observer*, 28 October 2007, website: www.guardian.co.uk/uk/2007/oct/28/britishidentity.society, accessed 2 May 2008

Holder, J, *It's (Not) Grim Up North*, BBC Books, 2005

Lonely Planet, *Lonely Planet Guide to Great Britain*, 6th edn, Lonely Planet, London, 2005

Office of the Deputy Prime Minister, House of Commons Report, 'Housing, Planning, Local Government and the Regions Committee: Reducing Regional Disparities in Prosperity', Ninth Report of Session 2002–03, Volume I: Report, website: www.publications.parliament.uk/pa/cm200203/cmselect/cmodpm/492/492.pdf, accessed 6 May 2008

Soreff, S M, 'Suicide', *E-medicine*, 2006, website: www.emedicine.com/MED/topic3004.htm, accessed 14 February 2008

The headache-prone woman

Lance, J, *Mechanism and Management of Headache*, 4th edn, p.182, Butterworth Scientific, London, 1982

Stewart, W F, Shechter, A, and Rasmussen, B K, 'Migraine prevalence: a review of population-based studies', *Neurology*, 44/4, S17–S23, 1994

The intelligent classical music lover

Bangerter, A, and Heath, C, 'The Mozart effect: tracking the evolution of a scientific legend', *British Journal of Social Psychology*, 43, 1–37, 2004

Campbell, D, *The Mozart Effect: Tapping the Power of Music to Heal the Body, Strengthen the Mind, and Unlock the Creative Spirit*, William Morrow and Co., USA, 1997

Chabris, C F, 'Prelude or requiem for the "Mozart effect"?' *Nature*, 400, 826–27, 1999

Hughes, J R, Daaboul, Y, Fino, J J, *et al.*, 'The Mozart effect on epileptiform activity', *Clinical Electroencephalography*, 29, 109–19, 1998

Jenkins, J S, 'The Mozart effect', *Journal of the Royal Society of Medicine*, 94, 170–2, 2001

Leng, X, and Shaw, G L, 'Toward a neural theory of higher brain function using music as a window', *Concepts in Neuroscience*, 2/2, 229–58, 1991

Nantais, K M, and Schellenberg, E G, 'The Mozart effect: an artefact of preference', *Psychological Science*, 10/4, 370–3, 1999

Rauscher, F H, 'The Mozart effect in rats: response to Steele', *Music Perception*, 23/5, 447–53, 2006

Rauscher, F H, Shaw, G L, and Ky, K N, 'Music and spatial task performance', *Nature*, 365, 611, 1993

Steele, K, 'Unconvincing evidence that rats show a Mozart effect', *Music Perception*, 23/5, 455–8, 2006

Thompson, W F, Schellenberg, E G, and Husain, G, 'Arousal, mood and the Mozart effect', *Psychological Science*, 12/3, 248–51, 2001

Wilson, T L, and Brown, T L, 'Re-examination of the effect of Mozart's music on spatial task performance', *Journal of Psychology*, 131/4, 365, 1997

The lazy fatty

Allison, D B, Basile, V C, and Yuker, H E, 'The measurement of attitudes toward and beliefs about obese persons', *International Journal of Eating Disorders*, 10, 599–607, 1991

Anesbury, T, and Tiggemann, M, 'An attempt to reduce negative stereotyping of obesity in children by changing controllability beliefs', *Health Education Research*, 15/2, 145–52, 2000

Cogan, J C, Bhalla, S K, Sefa-Dedeh, A, *et al.*, 'A comparison study of United States and African students on perceptions of obesity and thinness', *Journal of Cross-Cultural Psychology*, 27, 98–113, 1996

Crandall, C S, 'Prejudice against fat people: ideology and self-interest', *Journal of Personality and Social Psychology*, 66, 882–94, 1994

Crandall, C S, 'Do parents discriminate against their heavyweight daughters?', *Personality and Social Psychology Bulletin*, 21/7, 724–35, 1995

Crandall, C S, and Biernat, M, 'The ideology of anti-fat attitudes', *Journal of Applied Social Psychology*, 20, 227–43, 1990

Millman, M, *Such a Pretty Face: Being Fat in America*, Norton, New York, 1980

NAAFA, 2008, website: www.naafa org, accessed 8 January 2008

Nesse, R, 'How is Darwinian medicine useful?', *Western Journal of Medicine*, 174/5, 358–60, 2001

NHS Direct, website: www.nhsdirect.nhs.uk/articles/article.aspx?articleId=2 65&sectionId=32, accessed 4 January 2008

Rothblum, E D, 'I'll die for the revolution but don't ask me not to diet: feminism and the continuing stigmatization of obesity', in: Fallon, P, Katzman, M, and Wooley, S (Eds), *Feminist Perspectives on Eating Disorders*, Guilford Press, New York, 1993

Stunkard, A J, Foch, T T, and Hrubec, Z, 'A twin study of human obesity', *Journal of the American Medical Association*, 256, 51–4, 1986

Teachman, B A, and Brownell, K D, 'Implicit anti-fat bias among health professionals: is anyone immune?', *International Journal of Obesity and Related Metabolic Disorders*, 25/10, 1525–31, 2001

Tiggemann, M, and Rothblum, E D, 'Gender differences in social consequences of perceived overweight in the United States and Australia', *Sex Roles*, 18, 75–86, 1988

Turnbull, J D, Heaslip, S, and McLeod, H, 'Pre-school children's attitudes to fat and normal male and female stimulus figures', *International Journal of Obesity*, 24/12, 1705–06, 2000

Venturini, B, Castelli, L and Tomelleri, S, 'Not all jobs are suitable for fat people: experimental evidence of a link between being fat and "out-of-sight" jobs',

Social Behavior and Personality: An International Journal, 34/4, 389–98, 2006

Weiner, B, Perry, R P, and Magnusson, J, 'An attributional analysis of reactions to stigmas', *Journal of Personality and Social Psychology*, 55, 738–48, 1988

The lying politician

Centre for Policy Studies, *The 2008 Lexicon: A Guide to Contemporary Newspeak*, Centre for Policy Studies, London, 2008

DePaulo, B M, Kashy, D, Kirkendol, S E, *et al.*, 'Lying in everyday life', *Journal of Personality and Social Psychology*, 70, 979–95, 1996

Leadbeater, E, 'Why politicians cannot tell fibs', website: http://news.bbc.co.uk/go/pr/fr/–/1/hi/health/5316916.stm, Norwich, 5 September 2006, accessed 7 January 2008

Lock, C, 'Deception detection: psychologists try to learn how to spot a liar', *Science News*, 166/5, 72, 2004

Patterson, F, *Koko's Kitchen*, Scholastic Press, New York, 1987

Science Blog, 'Why we lie: because society tells us to', website: www.scienceblog. com/community/older/1996/A/199600023.html, Waltham, Massachusetts, 2004, accessed 7 January 2008

The mad genius

Carson, S, Peterson, J, and Higgins, D, 'Decreased latent inhibition is associated with increased creative achievement in high-functioning individuals', *Journal of Personality and Social Psychology*, 85/3, 499–506, 2003

Eliot, T S, 'Tradition and the individual talent II', *The Egoist*, 6/5, 72–3, 1919

Ellis, H, *A Study of British Genius*, revised edn, Houghton Mifflin, Boston, 1926

Eysenck, H J, *Genius: The Natural History of Creativity*, Cambridge University Press, New York, 1995

Jamison, K R, *Touched with Fire: Manic–Depressive Illness and the Artistic Temperament*, Free Press, New York, 1993

Ludwig, M, *The Price of Greatness: Resolving the Creativity and Madness Controversy*, Guilford Press, New York, 1995

Post, F, 'Creativity and psychopathology: a study of 291 world-famous men', *British Journal of Psychiatry*, 165/2, 22–34, 1994

Simeonova, D, Chang, K, Strong, C, *et al.*, 'Creativity in familial bipolar disorder', *Journal of Psychiatric Research*, 39/6, 623–31, 2005

Simonton, D K, *Creativity in Science: Chance, Logic, Genius, and Zeitgeist*, Cambridge University Press, New York, 2004

Simonton, D K, 'Are genius and madness related? Contemporary answers to an ancient question', *Psychiatric Times*, 22/7, 2005

The old fogey

Brodetsky, S, 'Newton: scientist and man', *Nature*, 150, 698–9, 1942

Cunningham, W R, and Brookbank, J W, *Gerontology: The Psychology, Biology, and Sociology of Aging*, Harper and Row, New York, 1988

Erikson, E, *Identity, Youth and Crisis*, Norton, New York, 1968

Kanazawa, S, 'Why productivity fades with age: the crime–genius connection', *Journal of Research in Personality*, 37, 257–72, 2003

Kelley, C L, and Charness, N, 'Issues in training older adults to use computers', *Behaviour and Information Technology*, 14/2, 107–20, 1995

Masters, W H, and Johnson, V E, *Human Sexual Inadequacy*, Churchill, London, 1970

Milgram, N W, Head, E, Zicker, S C, *et al.*, 'Learning ability in aged beagle dogs is preserved by behavioral enrichment and dietary fortification: a two-year longitudinal study', *Neurobiology of Aging*, 26/1, 77–90, 2005

The passionate redhead

BBC Scotland, 'Scots ginger nuts appeal', 4 July 2000, website: http://news. bbc.co.uk/1/low/scotland/819117.stm, accessed 22 May 2008

Branicki, W, Brudnik, U, Kupiec, T, *et al.*, 'Prediction of physical appearance based on genetic analysis is a very attractive prospect for forensic investigations', *Journal of Forensic Science*, 52/2, 349–54, 2007

Daily Mail, 'Redheads "have more sex than blondes or brunettes"', 15 August 2006, website: www.dailymail.co.uk/pages/live/articles/news/news. html?in_article_id=400779&in_page_id=1770, accessed 11 March 2008

Liem, E B, Joiner, T V, Tsueda, K, *et al.*, 'Increased sensitivity to thermal pain and reduced subcutaneous lidocaine efficacy in redheads', *Anesthesiology*, 102/3, 509–14, 2005

Mogil, J S, Ritchie, J, Smith, S B, *et al.*, 'Melanocortin-1 receptor gene variants affect pain and mu-opioid analgesia in mice and humans', *Journal of Medical Genetics*, 42/7, 583–7, 2005

Roach, M, *The Roots of Desire: The Myth, Meaning and Sexual Power of Red Hair*, Bloomsbury, London, 2005

Takeda, M B, Helms, M M, and Romanova, N, 'Hair Color Stereotyping and CEO Selection in the United Kingdom', *Journal of Human Behavior in the Social Environment: A Professional Journal*, 13/3, 85–99, 2006

Weir, S, and Fine-Davis, M, '"Dumb blonde" and "temperamental redhead"', *Irish Journal of Psychology*, 10, 11–19, 1989

The porn-obsessed man

BBC, 'The surgery: sex and relationships', website: www.bbc.co.uk/surgery/sex_relationships/sex/porn/, 2007, accessed 14 April 2008

Buss, D M, 'Sexual strategies theory: historical origins and current status', *Journal of Sex Research*, 35/1, 19–31, 1998

Carroll, J S, Padilla-Walker, L M, Nelson, L J, *et al.*, 'Generation XXX: pornography acceptance and use among emerging adults', *Journal of Adolescent Research*, 23, 6–30, 2008

Cooper, A, Mansson, S A, Daneback, K, *et al.*, 'Predicting the future of internet sex: online sexual activities in Sweden', *Sexual and Relationship Therapy*, 18/3, 277–91, 2003

Greenberg, B S, Brown, J D, and Buerke-Rothfuss, N L, *Media, Sex and the Adolescent*, Hampton Press, Cresskill, New Jersey, 1993

Kukkonen, T, Binik, Y, Amsel, R, *et al.*, 'Thermography as a physiological measure of sexual arousal in both men and women', *Journal of Sexual Medicine*, 4, 93–105, 2007

Malamuth, N M, 'Sexually explicit media, gender differences, and evolutionary theory', *Journal of Communication*, 46/3, 8–31, 1996

Marriott, E, 'Men and porn', *Guardian*, London, 8 November 2003, website: www.guardian.co.uk/world/2003/nov/08/gender.weekend7, accessed 8 January 2008

Ra'Anan, Z, and Sagi, A, 'Alternative mating strategies in male morphotypes of the freshwater prawn *Macrobrachium rosenbergii* (de Man)', *Biological Bulletin*, 169, 592–601, 1985

Williams, L, *Hard Core: Power, Pleasure and the Frenzy of the Visible*, Pandora Press, London, 1990

The promiscuous gay man

Bailey, J M, Gaulin, S, Agyei, Y, *et al.*, 'Effects of gender and sexual orientation on evolutionarily relevant aspects of human mating psychology', *Journal of Personality and Social Psychology*, 66, 1081–93, 1994

Billy, J O G, Tanfer, K, Grady, W R, *et al.*, 'The sexual behavior of men in the United States', *Family Planning Perspectives*, 25/2, 52–60, 1993

Binson, D, Michaels, S, Stall, R, *et al.*, 'Prevalence and social distribution of men who have sex with men: United States and its urban centers', *Journal of Sex Research*, 32, 245–54, 1995

Dolcini, M M, Catania, J A, Coates, T J, *et al.*, 'The National AIDS Behavioral Surveys (NABS)', *Family Planning Perspectives*, 25, 208–14, 1993

Fay, R, 'Prevalence and patterns of same-gender sexual contact among men', *Science*, 243, 338–48, 1989

Fisher, T, 'A response to David Glesne regarding promiscuity statistics in the context of his book *Understanding Homosexuality*', 2006, website: timrfisher. tripod.com/dgstats.htm#_1._Laumann_et., accessed 14 February 2008

Laumann, E O, Gagnon, J H, Michael, R, *et al.*, *The Social Organization of Sexuality: Sexual Practices in the United States*, University of Chicago Press, Chicago, 1994

Symons, D, *The Evolution of Human Sexuality*, Oxford University Press, New York, 1979

The sadistic prison guard

Goleman, D, 'The torturer's mind: complex view emerges', *New York Times*, 14 May 1985

Haney, C, Banks, W C, and Zimbardo, P G, 'A study of prisoners and guards in a simulated prison', *Naval Research Review*, 30, 4–17, 1973

Milgram, S, 'Behavioural study of obedience', *Journal of Abnormal and Social Psychology*, 67, 391–8, 1963

Zimbardo, P G, 'A situationist perspective on the psychology of evil: understanding how good people are transformed into perpetrators', in: Miller, A (Ed), *The Social Psychology of Good and Evil: Understanding our Capacity for Kindness and Cruelty*, Guilford Press, New York, 2004

Zimbardo, P G, *The Lucifer Effect: How Good People Turn Evil*, Rider and Co., UK, 2008

The schizophrenic with the split personality

ABC Science On-line, website: www.abc.net.au/science/articles/2004/09/16/1200266.htm?site=science/greatmomentsinscience&topic=health, 2004, accessed 5 May 2008

American Psychiatric Association (APA), *Diagnostic and Statistical Manual of Mental Disorders: DSM–IV*, 4th edn, American Psychiatric Association, Washington DC, 1994

Baron-Faust, R, 'Review: *Me, Myself and Irene*', *British Medical Journal*, 321, 770, 2000

BBC News, website: http://news.bbc.co.uk/go/pr/fr/–/1/hi/health/6033013.stm, 10 September 2006, accessed 11 January 2008

Chung, K F, and Chan, J H, 'Can a less pejorative Chinese translation for schizophrenia reduce stigma? A study of adolescents' attitudes toward people with schizophrenia', *Psychiatry and Clinical Neurosciences*, 58/5, 507, 2004

Gross, R, and Rolls, G, *Essential AS and A2 Psychology*, Hodder Education, London, 2006

Smith, A, and Cooper, S, 'Hollywood schizophrenia', *Student BMJ*, 14, 309–52, 2006, website: http://student.bmj.com/issues/06/09/life/346.php, accessed 13 January 2008

The sex-obsessed man

Brizendine, L, *The Female Brain*, Broadway, Doubleday Broadway Publishing Group, New York, 2006

Cameron, P, 'Note on time spent thinking about sex', *Psychological Reports*, 20, 741–2, 1967

Cameron, P, and Biber, H, 'Sexual thought throughout the lifespan', *Gerontologist*, 13, 144–7, 1973

Jones, J C, and Barlow, D H, 'Self-reported frequency of sexual urges, fantasies, and masturbatory fantasies in heterosexual males and females', *Archives of Sexual Behavior*, 19, 269–79, 1990

Laumann, E O, Gagnon, J H, Michael, R T, *et al.*, *The Social Organization of Sexuality*, University of Chicago, 1994

Leitenberg, H, and Henning, K, 'Sexual fantasy', *Psychological Bulletin*, 117, 469–96, 1995

Liberman, M, '"Every 52 seconds": wrong by 23,736 percent?' website: http://itre.cis.upenn.edu/~myl/languagelog/archives/003668.html, 13 October 2006, accessed 10 December 2007

The slim and seductive woman

Buss, D, *The Evolution of Desire*, Basic Books, New York, 2003

Freese, J, and Meland, S, 'Seven tenths incorrect: heterogeneity and change in the waist-to-hip ratios of *Playboy* centerfold models and Miss America winners', *Journal of Sex Research*, 39, 133–8, 2002

Pearl, A, Arroll, B, Lello, J, *et al.*, 'The impact of acne: a study of adolescents' attitudes, perception, and knowledge', *New Zealand Medical Journal*, 111, 269–71, 1998

Singh, D, 'Adaptive significance of female physical attractiveness: role of waist-to-hip ratio', *Journal of Personality and Social Psychology*, 65, 293–307, 1993

Singh, D, 'Is thin really beautiful and good? Relationship between waist-to-hip ratio (WHR) and female attractiveness', *Personality and Individual Differences*, 16, 123–32, 1994

Swami, V, Knight, D, Tovée, M, *et al.*, 'Preferences for female body size in Britain and the South Pacific', *Body Image*, 4, 2, 219–23, 2007

Symons, D, 'Beauty is in the adaptations of the beholder: the evolutionary psychology of human female sexual attractiveness', in: Ambramson, P R, and Pinkerton, S D (Eds), *Sexual Nature/Sexual Culture*, pp.80–118, University of Chicago Press, Chicago, 1995

Tovée, M J, Maizey, D S, Emery, J L, *et al.*, 'Visual cues to female physical attractiveness', *Proceedings of the Royal Society of London – B: Biological Science*, 266 (1415), 211–18, 1999

Wetsman, A, and Marlowe, F, 'How universal are preferences for female waist-to-hip ratios? Evidence from the Hadza of Tanzania – the role of genetics and adaptation', *Evolution and Human Behavior*, 20/4, 219–28, 1999

Yu, D W, and Shepard, G H, 'Is beauty in the eye of the beholder?', *Nature*, 396, 321–2, 1998

The slothful student

Levine, M, *The Myth of Laziness*, Simon and Schuster, USA, 2003

MacLeod, D, 'Time bomb', *Guardian*, 25 Sept 2007, website: http://education. guardian.co.uk/universityteachinginspection/story/0,,2176187,00.html, accessed 29 January 2008

Maslow, A, 'A theory of human motivation', *Psychological Review*, 50, 370–96, 1943

The sower of wild oats

Bailey, J M, Gaulin, S J C, Agyei, Y, *et al.*, 'Effects of gender and sexual orientation on evolutionarily relevant aspects of human mating psychology', *Journal of Personality and Social Psychology*, 66/6, 1081–93, 1994

Burley, N, and Symanski, R, 'Women without: an evolutionary and cross-cultural perspective on prostitution', in: Symanski, R (Ed), *The Immoral Landscape: Female Prostitution in Western Societies*, Butterworth and Co., Toronto, 1981

Buss, D M, *The Evolution of Desire*, Basic Books, New York, 1994

Buss, D M, and Schmitt, D P, 'Sexual strategies theory: an evolutionary perspective on human mating', *Psychological Review*, 100, 204–32, 1993

Clark, R D, 'The impact of AIDS on gender differences in willingness to engage in casual sex', *Journal of Applied Social Psychology*, 20, 771–82, 1990

Clark, R D, and Hatfield, E, 'Gender differences in receptivity to sexual offers', *Journal of Psychology and Human Sexuality*, 2, 39–55, 1989

Ellis, B J, and Symons, D, 'Sex differences in sexual fantasy: an evolutionary psychological approach', *Journal of Sex Research*, 27, 527–56, 1990

Kinsey, A C, Pomeroy, W B, and Martin, C E, *Sexual Behavior in the Human Male*, Saunders, Philadelphia, 1948

Okami, P, and Shackelford, T, 'Human sex differences in sexual psychology and behavior', *Annual Review of Sex Research*, 2001

Townsend, J M, 'Sex without emotional involvement: an evolutionary interpretation of sex differences', *Archives of Sexual Behavior*, 24, 171–204, 1995

Wilson, G, *The Great Sex Divide: A Study of Male–Female Differences*, Peter Owen, London, 1989

The stressed-out grey-haired person

Ballantyne, C, 'Fact or fiction? Stress causes gray hair', *Scientific American*, 24 October 2007

Hanjani, N M, and Cymet, T, 'Gray hair: medical explanations and issues', *Clinical Geriatrics*, 11/3, 36–42, 2003

Mosley, J G, and Gibbs, A C, 'Premature grey hair and hair loss among smokers: a new opportunity for health education?', *British Medical Journal*, 313, 1616, 1996

Schnohr, P, Nyboe, J, Lange, P, *et al*., 'Longevity and gray hair, baldness, facial wrinkles, and arcus senilis in 13,000 men and women: the Copenhagen City Heart Study', *Journals of Gerontology Series A: Biological Sciences and Medical Sciences*, 53/5, M347–50, 1998

The stupid WAG

Gross, R D, and Rolls, G, *Essential Psychology for AS and A2: For AQA(A)*, Hodder Arnold, London, 2006

The violent madman

Povey, D (Ed), *National Crime Statistics: Crime in England and Wales 2002/2003, Supplementary Volume 1: Homicide and Gun Crime*, January 2004

Rosenhan, D, 'On being sane in insane places', *Science*, 179, 250–8, 1973

Szasz, T S, *The Myth of Mental Illness*, Paladin, London, 1972

Tantum, D, 'The anti-psychiatry movement', in: Berrios, G E, and Freeman, H (Eds), *150 Years of British Psychiatry, 1841–1991*, Gaskell, London, 1991

Taylor, P J, and Gunn, J, 'Homicides by people with mental illness: myth and reality', *British Journal of Psychiatry*, 174, 9–14, 1999

The weaker sex

Cassen, R, and Kingdon, G, 'Tackling low educational achievement', website: www.jrf.org.uk/knowledge/findings/socialpolicy/2095.asp, Joseph Rowntree Foundation, York, June 2007, accessed 22 January 2008

Jones, M, 'The weaker sex', *New York Times*, 16 March 2003, website: http://query.nytimes.com/gst/fullpage.html?res=940CE6D8163EF935A25750C0A9659C8B63, accessed 21 January 2008

Keogh, E, 'Women feel more pain than men', website: www.medicalnewstoday.com/articles/26934.php, 2008, accessed 21 January 2008

Mitchell, L, MacDonald, R, and Brodie, E, 'Temperature and the cold pressor test', *Journal of Pain*, 5/4, 233–7, 2004

Observer, 'We've never had it so good', website: http://lifeandhealth.guardian.co.uk/family/story/0,,2028537,00.html, 11 March 2007, accessed 5 May 2008

Plant, M, 'Girls binge drinking more than boys', website: www.medicalnewstoday.com/articles/16995.php, 29 November 2004, accessed 22 January 2008

Sykes, B, *Adam's Curse: A Future Without Men*, Bantam Press, London, 2003

The wicked stepmother

Bettelheim, B, *The Uses of Enchantment: The Meaning and Importance of Fairy Tales*, Vintage, New York, 1989

Dainton, M, 'The myths and misconceptions of the stepmother identity', *Family Relations*, 42/1, 93–8, 1993

Daly, M, and Wilson, M I, 'Violence against stepchildren', *Psychological Science*, 5/3, 77–80, 1996

Doodson, L, and Morley, D, 'Understanding the roles of non-residential stepmothers', *Journal of Divorce and Remarriage*, 45/3–4, 109–30, 2006

Furstenberg, F, and Cherlin, A, *Divided Families: What Happens to Children When Parents Part*, Harvard University Press, 2006

Misrach, M, 'The wicked stepmother and other nasty myths', *Redbook*, July 1993

Pruett, C L, Calsyn, R J, and Jensen, F M, 'Social support received by children in stepmother, stepfather, and intact families', *Journal of Divorce and Remarriage*, 19/3–4, 165–80, 1993

Roesch, M, 'Wicked stepmothers: fact or fiction?', website: www.siskiyous.edu/class/engl12/stepmom.htm, 2007, accessed 6 January 2008

Rutter, V, 'Lessons from stepfamilies', *Psychology Today*, May/June 1994

Watson, P, *Ancient Stepmothers: Myth, Misogyny and Reality*, E J Brill, New York, 1995

The woman who can't park and the man who can't pack

The car parking video mentioned at the beginning of the chapter can be viewed at: www.youtube.com/watch?v=J8ANegTEqW4.

Berger, M L, 'Women drivers: the emergence of folklore and stereotypic opinions concerning feminine automotive behavior', *Women's Studies International Forum*, 9/3, 257–63, 1986

Maycock, G, Lockwood, C R, and Lester, J F, *The Accident Liability of Car Drivers*, Transport and Road Research Laboratory (TRRL) Report RR315, Crowthorne, 1991

Pease, A, and Pease, B, *Why Men Don't Listen and Women Can't Read Maps: How We're Different and What to Do About It'*, Orion, London, 2001

Reason, J T, Manstead, A S R, Stradling, S G, *et al.*, 'Errors and violations on the road: a real distinction?', *Ergonomics*, 33/10–11, 1315–32, 1990

St Louis Historical Society, website: www.slphistory.org/history/automilestones.asp, 2008, accessed 5 May 2008

Telegraph.co.uk, 'Why women have been on the road to nowhere', 2002, website: www.telegraph.co.uk/health/main.jhtml?xml=/health/2002/08/05/hside05.xml, accessed 7 January 2008

Also from Chambers:

taking the proverbial
the psychology of proverbs and sayings

Geoff Rolls

'An intriguing and original look at more than 60 sayings that will be essential reading'
The Guardian

Does familiarity breed contempt?
Are two heads better than one?
Is confession good for the soul?
If at first you don't succeed, should you really try again?

Taking the Proverbial answers these and many other questions with an engaging mix of humour and psychological insight, examining the truths and misconceptions behind the proverbs and sayings we use every day.

Author and psychology lecturer Geoff Rolls reveals why there may not be safety in numbers, how a gorilla can pass unnoticed on a basketball court and why people in lifts don't look at one another. Clever, compelling and often surprising, this is the perfect book for anyone who wants to find out more about why we behave the way we do.

ISBN: 978 0550 10335 2
Paperback
224pp
198×129mm

www.chambers.co.uk